Silent Slaves: The Dark Trade of Human Trafficking

John Shenton

Published by John Shenton, 2024.

While every precaution has been taken in the preparation of this book, the publisher assumes no responsibility for errors or omissions, or for damages resulting from the use of the information contained herein.

SILENT SLAVES: THE DARK TRADE OF HUMAN TRAFFICKING

First edition. October 27, 2024.

Copyright © 2024 John Shenton.

ISBN: 979-8227379498

Written by John Shenton.

Also by John Shenton

Business Plan Basics
The Bahamas - More Islands and Recipes Than You Expect!
Collected Musings from Bricks and Mortar to E-commerce
The Smart City Odyssey: Unveiling the Secrets to Traveller-Centric
Software
The Dragon's Gambit: China's Bid for Global Dominance and the
Western Response
Silent Weapon
Business Basics: Money Sources
Influx
Fried Chips
Mandates, Motors, and Misinformation
Echos of Orwell
Control and Chaos
The Empire's Warning: What Rome's Fall Tells Us About the West
Today
Silent Slaves: The Dark Trade of Human Trafficking

Table of Contents

Introduction

Human trafficking is one of the most pressing and insidious crises of our time, a dark stain on the modern world that has, for far too long, operated in the shadows. In my book, *Silent Slaves: The Dark Trade of Human Trafficking*, I seek to bring this underground world into the light. This book is more than just an account of the atrocities; it's a call to action, an appeal to conscience, and a roadmap toward solutions. I intend to provide a comprehensive exploration of human trafficking in Western countries, examining not only the global machinery behind this trade but also the heart-wrenching stories of the victims caught within it. From an in-depth analysis of traffickers' networks to the demand-driven markets that perpetrate these heinous crimes, this book seeks to lay bare the forces that sustain trafficking and to advocate for the policy reforms urgently needed to combat it.

This book's journey starts with a global overview, charting the history of human trafficking and the evolution of its methods from ancient slavery to the illicit practices of today. Despite progress in legal frameworks and international conventions, trafficking persists with alarming resilience, exploiting weak governance, social vulnerabilities, and often inadequate border controls. It's an illicit trade shaped by deep-seated societal issues: corruption, poverty, unchecked demand, and the dark side of digital connectivity. The persistence of trafficking, even in the face of stringent laws and robust advocacy efforts, suggests a need to rethink and bolster our response.

Each chapter of *Silent Slaves* unpacks different dimensions of this crisis, combining statistical analysis with real-life accounts. From examining the profiles of victims and traffickers to understanding the mechanics of organised crime networks, each page is dedicated to a specific aspect of trafficking, woven together to form a complete tapestry of a global issue with far-reaching implications. I hope that this book will not only educate but also spark dialogue on what can and must be done to curb trafficking in the West.

Chapter Highlights

The opening chapter, *Unveiling the Crisis: A Global Overview of Human Trafficking*, sets the stage for the entire book by providing a contextual foundation. It charts the historical roots of human trafficking and underscores its transformation over the centuries. With a data-driven perspective, I map out trafficking flows into the USA, Europe, and other Western nations, demonstrating how trafficking has expanded, morphed, and adapted in response to enforcement efforts. Here, I introduce international laws like the Palermo Protocol, setting the groundwork for later critiques on the efficacy of legal responses to trafficking.

Moving through the chapters, readers encounter a vivid portrayal of the trafficking victims, each profile offering a haunting reminder of the human lives affected. In *Profiles of the Victims: Who Are They?* I examine who these individuals are and how they are manipulated and drawn into exploitation. This chapter places particular emphasis on the vulnerabilities of those trafficked: refugees, economic migrants, and those from impoverished backgrounds. I aim to provide a face to the faceless numbers, an empathetic connection that will underscore the importance of every life affected.

I also examine *The Machinery of Trafficking: Organised Crime Networks*, which dissects the operational systems traffickers use. From powerful international syndicates to regional criminal organisations, these networks function with the ruthless efficiency of any multinational corporation, driven by financial incentives that far outweigh the risks they face. Through these chapters, I lay bare how traffickers exploit the legal and governance gaps across borders and how corruption oils the machinery of trafficking, as seen in *The Role of Corruption: How Governance and Law Enforcement Fail.*

The Role of Western Demand

One of the most difficult truths this book confronts is the role of demand within Western societies. In *The Western Demand: Sex, Labour, and Exploitation*, I probe into the uncomfortable reality that the demand for cheap labour and commercialised sex sustains this dark trade. Western nations often focus on the supply side, attempting to dismantle trafficking networks and prosecute traffickers, but this approach overlooks the very forces that create and drive demand. This chapter considers sectors where exploitation is particularly rife agriculture, construction, domestic service, and the commercial sex industry and calls on Western consumers and governments alike to recognise their role in fuelling trafficking.

The Future of Anti-Trafficking Efforts

As the book progresses towards a resolution, I present *Towards a Solution: Policy Recommendations and Future Directions*. This final chapter represents the heart of my message a call to action that no single nation can achieve alone. I explore policy recommendations designed to tackle trafficking at every level, from tightening border controls and reforming immigration policies to ensuring more robust international cooperation. Recognising that traffickers are adept at exploiting inconsistencies across borders, I propose initiatives that emphasise a unified approach, allowing countries to share intelligence, close legal loopholes, and present a stronger front against traffickers.

Further, I argue that addressing the demand side of trafficking is as crucial as targeting traffickers themselves. I outline suggestions for public education campaigns that aim to dissuade consumers from supporting exploitative industries and encourage businesses to scrutinise their supply chains for ethical compliance. This chapter also underscores the need for a victim-centred approach, advocating for policies that provide real support to trafficking survivors that extends beyond rescue to include psychological, social, and economic reintegration.

Silent Slaves offers not only a condemnation of human trafficking but also a vision of how we might eventually bring this inhumane trade to an end. However, it is a vision that demands global cooperation, consistent vigilance, and the willingness to confront uncomfortable truths about our societies and economies. As I lay out the frameworks and strategies for dismantling trafficking networks, I'm reminded that each victim rescued and each trafficker prosecuted represents a hard-fought step forward.

A Multi-Faceted Crisis with Global Stakes

Human trafficking is, at its core, a crisis of humanity, and I have structured this book to convey the gravity of this issue while offering pathways for change. Each chapter addresses a critical component of this dark trade, from the individual victims to the systemic enablers, providing a detailed view that underscores trafficking as a global atrocity requiring a global response.

In writing *Silent Slaves: The Dark Trade of Human Trafficking*, I have sought to confront the painful realities of trafficking while offering hope through proposed solutions. This book is not merely an exploration but a plea for readers, policymakers, and societies to unite against this modern-day form of slavery. Together, by tackling trafficking from every angle, we can hope to end the silent suffering of those caught within its web and work towards a world where freedom, dignity, and humanity are truly universal rights.

Chapter 1: Unveiling the Crisis: A Global Overview of Human Trafficking

Human trafficking is, without a doubt, one of the gravest humanitarian crises of our time. It is a form of modern-day slavery that continues to thrive in the shadows, silently devastating millions of lives across the globe. As we embark on an exploration of this dark phenomenon, it is essential to understand the complexity and vastness of human trafficking, how it has evolved, and the frameworks in place that seek to eradicate it. This chapter serves as the foundation for a deeper investigation into the ways this nefarious trade infiltrates Western nations, including the USA and Europe, and how global policies and legal frameworks like the Palermo Protocol attempt to combat it.

The Evolution of Human Trafficking: From Ancient Slavery to Modern Exploitation

Slavery, in its various forms, is as old as recorded human history itself. From the early civilisations of Mesopotamia to the vast empires of Rome, Egypt, and Greece, slavery was an institutionalised and accepted practice. Human beings were bought, sold, and treated as property, their worth determined not by their humanity, but by their labour and servitude. Whether it was through war, debt, or birth, countless men, women, and children found themselves shackled into lives of forced labour and exploitation.

The transatlantic slave trade, perhaps the most infamous chapter in this historical narrative, witnessed the brutal transportation of millions of Africans to the Americas, where they were condemned to work in plantations under inhumane conditions. Though it was abolished in the 19th century, the vestiges of slavery never fully disappeared. Instead, they morphed and adapted, lurking in the shadows of legal progress.

In the contemporary era, human trafficking represents the latest iteration of this ancient exploitation. However, it has become far more clandestine and insidious, facilitated by globalisation, advancements in communication, and the ease of cross-border movement. Human trafficking today operates within a vast underground network, fuelled by organised crime syndicates, corrupt officials, and even individual opportunists who seek to profit from the desperation of vulnerable populations. Unlike historical slavery, which was often highly visible, entrenched in law, and practised openly within societies, modern human trafficking operates in more insidious ways. Traffickers exploit gaps within the global economy by disguising their activities under the veneer of legitimate businesses such as agriculture, manufacturing, or hospitality. Corrupt legal systems offer little protection, allowing traffickers to operate with relative impunity, while porous borders provide them access to vulnerable individuals, facilitating illegal movement across countries. This covert nature allows trafficking to persist undetected, making it even harder to combat than historical slavery.

Traffickers use legitimate supply chains or work within industries that rely on outsourced labour to exploit individuals under the guise of employment opportunities. Corruption further aids in concealing the crime, where officials may be bribed to look the other way, thus embedding trafficking operations within the legal frameworks meant to stop them. This fusion of legitimate and illicit operations not only hinders identification but also poses significant challenges for law enforcement to dismantle trafficking rings effectively.

Open border policies exacerbate this situation, providing an entry point for victims who are moved across regions with ease. For traffickers, these borders present an opportunity to evade law enforcement by shuttling individuals across jurisdictions, making detection and prosecution difficult. Many victims may also lack official documentation, becoming invisible within a legal system that fails to protect them, thereby entrapping them in a cycle of exploitation. Without the systemic visibility of historic slavery, modern trafficking thrives in the shadows, becoming a pervasive threat to vulnerable populations worldwide.

Defining Human Trafficking: A Global Problem with Local Manifestations

Human trafficking is generally defined as the recruitment, transportation, harbouring, or receipt of persons utilizing force, fraud, or coercion for exploitation. This exploitation can take many forms, including forced labour, sexual slavery, domestic servitude, organ trafficking, and child soldiering. Traffickers often target individuals who are vulnerable due to economic hardship, lack of education, political instability, or social isolation, manipulating or coercing them into situations from which escape is nearly impossible.

Trafficking does not respect borders. While it is true that certain regions act as hotspots for the recruitment and exploitation of victims, the reality is that every country is affected by human trafficking in some form either as a source, transit, or destination point. For Western nations like the USA and European countries, the influx of trafficked persons is a growing concern. Traffickers exploit vulnerable migrants and refugees, preying upon their hopes for a better life only to trap them in cycles of abuse and exploitation upon arrival.

The Scale of the Crisis: Statistical Insights

The scope of human trafficking is staggering, yet the true extent of the problem remains obscured by its clandestine nature. According to the International Labour Organization (ILO), there are an estimated 50 million people worldwide living in modern slavery, of whom approximately 27.6 million are in situations of forced labour, and 22 million are trapped in forced marriages. It is important to note that these figures are conservative estimates, as human trafficking is notoriously underreported.

In the United States, human trafficking is a significant and growing problem. Annually, an estimated 199,000 incidents are reported, according to the Department of Homeland Security. Victims often originate from both domestic and international locations, with many trafficked across the southern border or lured through deceptive job opportunities abroad. Trafficking rings frequently exploit vulnerabilities by promising work or safety, only to entrap individuals into forced labour or sexual exploitation.

In the United States, sex trafficking is the most prevalent form of human trafficking. Alarmingly, child sexual abuse material (CSAM) continues to grow at an exponential rate, with over 88 million reported files in 2022 alone. Child sex trafficking has been reported in all 50 U.S. states, highlighting the magnitude of this crisis. Globally, the human trafficking industry generates approximately $150 billion annually, making it one of the most profitable illegal enterprises. It is estimated that between 15,000 to 50,000 women and children are forced into sexual slavery in the United States every year, and the total number varies wildly as it is very difficult to research. One study from the Department of Health and Human Services estimated the number between 240,000 and 325,000, while a report from the University of Pennsylvania put it at between 100,000 and 300,000.

Social media and technological advancements have given traffickers new tools for recruitment, allowing them to exploit individuals, particularly minors. It is estimated that 500,000 predators are online daily, and many children are exposed to social media by the age of five. Disturbingly, one-third of these children are expected to face some form of online sexual harm before they turn 18.

Europe is also facing a similar crisis, with traffickers targeting vulnerable migrants and refugees, including many from conflict zones, as prime victims.

European countries, particularly those in the EU, have developed comprehensive anti-trafficking frameworks, yet enforcement remains lacklustre. The EU's open-border policies, while designed to promote the free movement of people, have inadvertently created conditions that traffickers exploit. Traffickers can move victims across borders with minimal detection, utilizing weak bureaucratic oversight, which varies across nations. This undermines enforcement efforts, as inconsistent cooperation among EU states results in gaps that traffickers exploit. Migrants, especially those lacking legal status, are the most vulnerable, as traffickers take advantage of their precarious situation.

The Schengen Zone's policy of eliminating border controls between many European nations has facilitated easier transportation for traffickers. While meant to foster economic integration and open societies, the system lacks sufficient safeguards for monitoring illegal activities within its borders. Traffickers exploit the policy's vulnerabilities, moving victims swiftly across multiple countries before law enforcement can effectively intervene. In some cases, this freedom of movement is exacerbated by corrupt local officials or overloaded migration systems, particularly in countries bordering major entry points into Europe.

Moreover, EU bureaucratic delays in addressing the growing complexities of migration and trafficking have further weakened the effectiveness of anti-trafficking policies. Law enforcement agencies, already strained by the challenges of migration, often lack the resources to fully investigate trafficking cases. This inconsistency in resources and training across EU states leads to a low prosecution rate, allowing traffickers to operate with near impunity. Human rights organizations have repeatedly criticized this fragmented approach, noting that while legislation exists, its patchy enforcement and lack of cross-border collaboration provide little deterrence to traffickers.

Migrants, especially those fleeing conflict zones or economic desperation, are particularly vulnerable under these conditions. Traffickers prey on these individuals, offering false promises of safety, employment, or asylum, only to exploit them once they cross the border. Many of these migrants, lacking proper documentation or awareness of their legal rights, find themselves trapped in a cycle of exploitation, with limited avenues for recourse in unfamiliar countries.

The complexity of modern trafficking, combined with bureaucratic inefficiencies and open-border policies, presents an ongoing challenge for European governments, leaving millions of migrants at risk of falling into the hands of traffickers.

War in Ukraine

The war in Ukraine has escalated human trafficking concerns, as the displacement of over 8 million people has created fertile ground for traffickers to exploit those fleeing conflict. Traffickers have seized on the chaos, targeting vulnerable women, children, and men for forced labour, sexual exploitation, and organ trafficking. According to the United Nations Office on Drugs and Crime (UNODC), women and children make up nearly 70% of trafficking victims globally, with sexual exploitation becoming alarmingly prevalent.

UNODC reports highlight that in conflict zones, such as Ukraine, traffickers use the vulnerability caused by displacement to recruit victims under the guise of offering safe passage, employment, or asylum. These victims often end up in forced labour camps, brothels, or other exploitative situations. For instance, in 2023, numerous reports emerged of women and children from Ukraine being trafficked into forced prostitution or domestic servitude, particularly in nearby European nations.

The complexity of trafficking across borders, compounded by the legal loopholes caused by differing national laws, has worsened the situation. International organizations have struggled to coordinate enforcement across jurisdictions, leading to uneven results in combating trafficking. Criminal networks operating in these zones often exploit these legal inconsistencies to continue their operations undeterred.

In addition to the socio-political instability brought on by war, the economic desperation faced by displaced populations drives both the demand and supply of trafficked individuals. Traffickers prey on these socio-economic vulnerabilities, presenting false job opportunities or immigration help, leading to entrapment. In Europe, rising poverty rates and reduced economic opportunities have fueled the demand for cheap labour and illicit services, driving the exploitation of displaced Ukrainians and other migrants.

In response to this crisis, anti-trafficking organizations, along with governmental bodies in Europe, have ramped up efforts to combat this issue. However, the sheer scale of displacement and the complexity of cross-border trafficking operations mean that international cooperation is essential to fully addressing the crisis. Increased border surveillance, better victim identification programs, and comprehensive legal reforms are needed to prevent traffickers from continuing to exploit the vulnerable amidst such conflicts.

As war continues to displace millions, the international community faces a daunting challenge: balancing the provision of humanitarian aid with the prevention of human trafficking, ensuring that fleeing populations do not fall prey to an increasingly sophisticated and global criminal network.

A Global Crisis

In 2024, human trafficking remains an urgent global crisis. Over 49.6 million individuals are entrapped in modern slavery today, with over 12 million of them being children. The root causes of this exploitation include economic hardship, psychological vulnerability, political instability, and natural disasters. Traffickers often manipulate their victims through force, fraud, or coercion, exploiting them for forced labour, sex, or domestic servitude.

The International Labour Organization now estimates that **27.6 million people** are victims of human trafficking globally. This includes **forced labour**, **sexual exploitation**, and **forced marriages**. In the United States, the estimated **199,000 annual cases** still reflect a severe underreporting issue. Many victims are trafficked across the southern border, while others are lured from abroad under pretences.

Victims often hail from Eastern Europe, Africa, and Asia, while Western European nations serve as prime markets. Efforts like the Palermo Protocol and various EU directives aim to combat this, but enforcement remains uneven across member states, hindered by differing legal frameworks and resource constraints.

Human trafficking is thus a transnational challenge that demands coordinated international action to combat both its root causes and its devastating effects on individuals and societies.

Trafficking routes often mirror traditional migration pathways, with Eastern Europe, Southeast Asia, and Central and South America serving as major source regions. Migrants from these regions, particularly those fleeing conflict, poverty, and environmental disasters, become easy targets for traffickers. In some instances, organised criminal networks operate within these communities, offering transportation and falsified documentation in exchange for a high price only to force these individuals into exploitation upon arrival in their destination country.

International Response: The Palermo Protocol and Other Key Frameworks

Recognising the global nature of human trafficking, the international community has taken several steps to combat this crisis. One of the most significant milestones in this effort was the adoption of the **Palermo Protocol** in 2000. Officially known as the **Protocol to Prevent, Suppress and Punish Trafficking in Persons, especially Women and Children**, this landmark treaty forms part of the broader United Nations Convention against Transnational Organized Crime. Its primary objectives are to:

- Prevent and combat human trafficking.
- Protect and assist the victims of trafficking
- Promote cooperation among nations to meet these goals

The Palermo Protocol was the first international instrument to define human trafficking and establish a comprehensive framework for its prevention. It obligates signatories to criminalise human trafficking, adopt measures to protect victims, and enhance cooperation across borders. Today, 178 countries are parties to the protocol, making it a crucial element of global anti-trafficking efforts.

In addition to the Palermo Protocol, several other international conventions and frameworks have emerged to combat trafficking. The **Council of Europe's Convention on Action against Trafficking in Human Beings**, adopted in 2005, aims to strengthen protections for victims and improve cooperation between member states. The **ILO Forced Labour Protocol** (2014) also emphasises measures to prevent trafficking and ensure the protection and compensation of victims.

Despite these frameworks, implementation varies widely, and many nations still struggle to enforce anti-trafficking laws effectively.

The Challenges of Enforcement and Prosecution

While international protocols like Palermo have laid the foundation for global cooperation, the enforcement of anti-trafficking laws remains fraught with challenges. In many countries, human trafficking is treated as a low-priority crime, and investigations often fall short due to a lack of resources or political will. Corruption, particularly in source and transit countries, exacerbates the problem, as traffickers bribe officials to overlook illegal activity or actively participate in the trade.

Moreover, prosecution rates remain alarmingly low. Trafficking cases are notoriously difficult to prosecute because victims are often reluctant to come forward due to fear of reprisals, lack of trust in authorities, or being entangled in their traffickers' networks. As a result, many traffickers operate with impunity, further emboldening their efforts.

The Way Forward: Laying the Foundation for Future Chapters

As we move forward in this exploration of human trafficking, it is important to keep in mind the deep-rooted historical context from which this trade arises. Slavery and exploitation, though they have shifted form, have been constants in human civilisation. Human trafficking today is merely the latest mutation of an age-old crime, one that flourishes amidst the modern complexities of globalisation, migration, poverty, and corruption.

To combat this crisis, various international efforts have emerged, including those led by the United Nations and the International Labour Organization, which work alongside local law enforcement agencies. The U.S. government, through the Trafficking Victims Protection Act and the annual Trafficking in Persons (TIP) Report, plays a key role in fighting human trafficking domestically and internationally. However, the numbers reveal an urgent need for more coordinated global efforts.

But opening borders to mass illegal migration has only exacerbated the problems.

Chapter 2: The Routes to Exploitation: How Victims are Trafficked into the West

In this chapter, I will explore the treacherous and ever-evolving routes that human traffickers use to smuggle victims into Western nations. These routes are not fixed; they adapt and shift according to enforcement efforts, geopolitical situations, and local vulnerabilities in both the source and destination countries. By examining the complex land, sea, and air pathways, I aim to shed light on how traffickers exploit human beings for profit, while law enforcement agencies struggle to keep pace with their evolving tactics.

The Global Web of Human Smuggling Networks

Human trafficking is a multi-billion-dollar industry, fuelled by a complex network of criminal organisations operating across multiple continents. From rural villages to bustling metropolises, traffickers prey on the vulnerable, luring victims with promises of better lives or simply abducting them by force. The routes to exploitation extend far beyond the geographical boundaries of any single country; they traverse entire regions, cutting across international borders, and exploiting both legal and illegal means of entry.

Traffickers operate out of various hot spots around the globe, with concentrations of activity in Africa, Eastern Europe, Latin America, and parts of Asia. These regions serve as the primary sources of victims, while the West particularly the USA, the UK, and European nations remains the destination for a significant portion of those trafficked. However, the routes used to transport these victims are as varied as the traffickers themselves, ranging from well-organised networks that function like professional logistics operations to smaller, more fragmented groups that thrive on chaos and corruption.

Land Routes: Crossings of Desperation

Land routes are a predominant means by which traffickers move their human cargo into Western countries. These routes are most visible at borders where poverty, conflict, or political instability force people to migrate in search of safety or opportunity an environment in which traffickers easily thrive.

In Eastern Europe, for instance, trafficking routes often originate in countries like Moldova, Ukraine, and the Balkans, where economic hardship creates a ready supply of potential victims. From these regions, victims are smuggled through neighbouring countries into Western Europe, often via the porous borders of nations with weak law enforcement capabilities. These routes may take them through Hungary, Poland, or Slovakia, eventually reaching wealthier EU countries such as Germany, France, and the UK, where demand for illicit labour or sexual exploitation is high. The traffickers rely on a combination of bribery, corruption, and false documents to move their victims through these borders undetected.

In Latin America, the trafficking routes converge towards the USA's southern border, a focal point for smuggling activities. From countries like Honduras, Guatemala, and El Salvador, victims are often transported by land through Mexico, enduring brutal conditions along the way. The US-Mexico border stands as both a symbol of hope and a stark reminder of the challenges that mass migration and trafficking bring. It represents the desperation of those fleeing poverty, violence, and political instability, but it also embodies the reality of a border under siege by traffickers and organised criminal networks. In recent years, under the current US administration, policies that have led to a more permissive approach towards migration have exacerbated the crisis. The opening of the border, combined with the lack of stringent checks or sufficient resources to manage the influx, has created a perfect storm for human traffickers.

The situation at the border is dire. Established trafficking routes, once used sparingly by organised crime syndicates, have now become bustling corridors for the mass smuggling of both illegal immigrants and trafficking victims. Traffickers exploit gaps in border enforcement, particularly in remote desert regions, where surveillance is weaker. They avoid official border crossings, knowing that those areas are more heavily monitored by Border Patrol and equipped with technology designed to detect and apprehend illegal crossings. Instead, they navigate treacherous terrain, leading their victims often women and children through remote areas where the threat of exposure to the elements, dehydration, and death is high. For traffickers, these human beings are mere commodities, and the risk to life is inconsequential.

A critical factor that amplifies the problem is the direct involvement of Mexican drug cartels, which have diversified their illicit activities beyond narcotics into human trafficking and smuggling. Cartels such as the Sinaloa and Jalisco New Generation Cartel (CJNG) have developed sophisticated smuggling networks, effectively controlling large stretches of the border. Their dominance allows them to charge migrants, many of whom have no other option but to pay exorbitant fees, for a chance to cross. In some cases, individuals are coerced into trafficking themselves to pay off these debts, with promises of freedom upon completion of dangerous or illegal tasks on behalf of the cartel.

The "coyotes," or human smugglers, often work under the auspices of these cartels. They use brutal methods to keep their human cargo in line, threatening, extorting, and abusing them. For those who cannot pay, or for whom the cartel sees an opportunity for additional profit, trafficking into forced labour or sexual exploitation becomes the grim alternative. Many women and children trafficked across the border are sold into prostitution, kept in captivity in the USA or distributed into sex trafficking rings that stretch across the country. Cartels and traffickers understand that the current administrative policies have reduced deterrents, creating a window of opportunity to expand their operations.

What is particularly alarming is the sheer volume of people being smuggled. The current administration's policies have resulted in a system where traffickers have seized the narrative of an "open border," encouraging a surge of migrants from Central America, Mexico, and even as far as Africa and the Middle East. While many are genuine asylum seekers, fleeing dangerous conditions, traffickers embed themselves within these migrant groups, using the chaos to conceal their activities. The overwhelmed immigration system cannot possibly vet every individual adequately, resulting in traffickers and their victims slipping through undetected.

The lack of rigorous checks and balances has turned the border into a trafficking hotspot. Traffickers have learned to exploit loopholes, such as the release of migrants into the US interior pending immigration hearings that may take months or even years to occur. In the meantime, many victims disappear into the shadows, forced into labour or sexual exploitation, and never reach the hearings for which they were originally scheduled. Without proper oversight, traffickers continue to thrive under these conditions, and the victims they smuggle remain trapped in a nightmare, invisible to the very system meant to protect them.

Additionally, the overwhelming number of people crossing the border has placed an immense strain on both federal and state law enforcement agencies. Border Patrol, Immigration and Customs Enforcement (ICE), and other governmental bodies are stretched thin, struggling to handle not just the large influx of migrants but also the growing presence of traffickers who have become more emboldened under the current environment. Law enforcement simply lacks the manpower, resources, and political support to adequately counteract the traffickers' increasingly complex operations. As a result, traffickers can adapt, moving their operations away from heavily guarded areas and focusing on the more vulnerable, less patrolled regions.

This unchecked mass migration, under the guise of asylum or economic migration, has allowed traffickers to embed themselves within legitimate migratory flows, making it nearly impossible for authorities to distinguish between genuine refugees and those being trafficked or involved in criminal enterprises. The traffickers take full advantage of the current administration's lack of a cohesive strategy to secure the border, exacerbating an already dire humanitarian crisis.

In conclusion, the US-Mexico border serves as a striking example of how permissive policies, when not coupled with robust enforcement, can become a gateway for human trafficking. The current administration's approach, which has opened the border to mass influx without sufficient checks or balances, has allowed traffickers to exploit the system, further victimising the vulnerable. Smuggling organisations and cartels have turned this opportunity into a lucrative business, and until significant changes are made to address the issue, the flow of trafficked individuals will only continue to grow. As the West faces an ever-growing influx of migrants and trafficking victims, it becomes clear that stronger enforcement, international cooperation, and a more comprehensive immigration policy are crucial if we are to protect the most vulnerable from exploitation and stop this modern-day slave trade.

Migrants attempting to escape violence and poverty become easy prey for traffickers, who use coercion, false promises, and threats to push them into forced labour or sexual exploitation once they reach US soil.

Sea Routes: The Perilous Journey Across the Mediterranean

Sea routes present some of the most hazardous conditions for trafficking victims, particularly those attempting to reach Europe via the Mediterranean. North Africa has long been a major hub for trafficking, with countries like Libya and Tunisia serving as launch points for boats carrying desperate migrants and trafficking victims towards Southern Europe, particularly Italy, Greece, and Spain.

The Mediterranean has become a graveyard for many who attempt the crossing. Smugglers often overload small, unseaworthy vessels with dozens, if not hundreds, of people, knowing full well that many will not survive the journey. For traffickers, these victims are nothing more than disposable cargo, and the risk to life is irrelevant. The collapse of the Libyan state following the fall of Muammar Gaddafi in 2011 has dramatically worsened the human trafficking crisis in North Africa, transforming Libya into a lawless breeding ground for traffickers, armed militias, and criminal networks. Under Gaddafi's rule, Libya functioned as a sort of gatekeeper for Europe, tightly controlling its borders and managing the flow of migrants through the country. His regime, though authoritarian and repressive in many ways, maintained a degree of stability that limited the scope of human trafficking operations. However, after his fall, Libya descended into chaos, and the ensuing power vacuum left the country fragmented, with competing militias and warlords vying for control. This instability, coupled with Libya's strategic position on the Mediterranean, has created fertile ground for traffickers to flourish.

In the absence of a functioning central government, traffickers and smugglers have turned Libya into a hub for human exploitation, where people desperate to reach Europe are routinely trapped in a nightmarish cycle of abuse. The borders, once closely monitored, are now wide open, allowing traffickers to operate with impunity. Libya's coastal cities, such as Tripoli, Zawiya, and Sabratha, have become epicentres for human trafficking, with thousands of migrants passing through these regions on their way to Europe.

Detention Centres and Camps: Exploitation Before the Journey Begins

One of the most harrowing aspects of the trafficking crisis in Libya is the situation within the numerous detention centres and makeshift camps that dot the country. These centres are ostensibly used to detain migrants attempting to make the crossing to Europe, but in reality, they have become lawless enclaves where abuse, violence, and exploitation are rampant. Many of these detention facilities are run by militias, which use them as opportunities for extortion and enslavement. Migrants who are intercepted or captured while attempting to cross the Mediterranean are often thrown into these camps, where they are held indefinitely, without any legal recourse, access to basic services, or protection from abuse.

Reports from various international organisations and human rights groups paint a grim picture of the conditions within these centres. Migrants face severe overcrowding, with hundreds of people packed into small spaces without access to clean water, proper sanitation, or adequate food supplies. Diseases spread quickly, and medical care is virtually non-existent. But beyond the squalid conditions, what is most shocking is the routine violence and exploitation to which these migrants are subjected. Many are beaten, tortured, and raped by their captors, who use violence as a means of control and intimidation. These abuses are not isolated incidents but are widespread and systematic, with traffickers and militias treating human beings as commodities to be bought, sold, and exploited.

Women and children are particularly vulnerable in these environments. Female migrants are frequently subjected to sexual violence, and many are forced into prostitution by their captors. In some cases, women are sold outright to traffickers who specialise in sex trafficking, turning them into commodities in an international trafficking market that spans from Libya to Europe and beyond. Children, too, are not spared from this horrific cycle. Young boys are often forced into labour, while young girls face a similar fate to women, either sold into prostitution or trafficked across the Mediterranean for exploitation in Europe.

A Profitable Trade for Militia Groups

In the absence of a centralised government, militias have become the dominant power in Libya, controlling key areas of the country and engaging in a range of illicit activities to fund their operations. Human trafficking has become one of the most lucrative businesses for these militias. They have transformed trafficking into an organised trade, profiting from every stage of the migrant's journey from their capture and detention to their sale to traffickers, and finally, to their eventual journey across the Mediterranean.

The militias, often linked to criminal gangs, operate with complete impunity. They control the vast desert regions where migrants enter Libya, often travelling from sub-Saharan Africa or neighbouring North African countries. These migrants are captured by armed groups or handed over by smugglers, and they are held in detention centres where they are forced to pay bribes or endure forced labour to buy their freedom. Those who cannot pay are often sold into slavery or trafficked into prostitution. In many cases, the militia groups work hand-in-hand with traffickers, treating migrants as a form of currency in the wider human trafficking market.

Once a migrant has paid off their captors, either through forced labour, ransom payments from relatives, or other forms of extortion, they are then sold to the next group of traffickers responsible for their journey across the Mediterranean. This system ensures that migrants are passed through multiple layers of exploitation before they ever even set foot on a boat, each stage representing another profit point for the militias and traffickers involved.

The Mediterranean: A Deadly Crossing

For those who survive the ordeal of the detention centres and camps, the next stage of the journey is often just as perilous: the crossing of the Mediterranean Sea. Libya's coast is now one of the primary departure points for boats carrying migrants to Europe, particularly Italy. The collapse of the Libyan state has meant that the coastline is largely unmonitored, and traffickers can operate freely, sending boat after boat towards Europe with little fear of being intercepted by Libyan authorities.

The boats used by traffickers are often overcrowded, unseaworthy, and barely able to withstand the conditions of the open sea. Traffickers cram as many people as possible into these small vessels, knowing that the chances of survival are slim, but caring little for the fate of those on board. For them, the human cargo is a means to an end, and if a boat capsizes or sinks, they simply send another. The migrants, many of whom have already endured unimaginable suffering, face the very real possibility of drowning at sea.

Despite the efforts of European naval patrols and humanitarian organisations, the sheer number of boats attempting the crossing makes it impossible to prevent all of them from setting off. The Mediterranean has become a graveyard for thousands of migrants, with those who drown becoming faceless statistics in the broader trafficking crisis. For those who do manage to reach European shores, many are intercepted and sent back to Libya, where the cycle of exploitation and abuse begins anew.

International Efforts and the Failure of Containment

In response to the growing crisis, the European Union and other international actors have implemented policies aimed at containing the flow of migrants from Libya. This has included funding for Libyan coastguards to intercept boats, partnerships with local authorities to combat trafficking, and efforts to improve conditions within the detention centres. However, these efforts have largely been ineffective in curbing the crisis. The Libyan coastguard, often poorly equipped and underfunded, has struggled to maintain control over the vast stretches of coastline. Moreover, many elements within the Libyan coastguard are themselves complicit in trafficking, further undermining the credibility of these international partnerships.

The failure of containment efforts is not just a logistical issue but also a moral one. By funding and supporting local forces that are complicit in the trafficking trade, the international community has been accused of indirectly fuelling the very crisis it seeks to solve. Migrants intercepted by the Libyan coastguard are often returned to the same detention centres where they face exploitation, creating a vicious cycle of abuse. Moreover, the focus on preventing migrants from reaching Europe has done little to address the root causes of migration or the rampant trafficking operations within Libya itself.

The collapse of the Libyan state following Gaddafi's fall has created a humanitarian disaster that extends beyond Libya's borders. The country has become a lawless haven for traffickers and militias, who profit from the desperation of migrants seeking a better life. For those trapped in Libya's detention centres and camps, the dream of reaching Europe is often met with a brutal reality of violence, exploitation, and trafficking. The international community's efforts, while well-intentioned, have failed to address the deeper structural issues that allow trafficking to thrive in Libya, and if the country remains in a state of chaos, the suffering of migrants will continue unabated.

The perilous journey migrants face across the Mediterranean Sea has a striking parallel with the dangerous crossings of the English Channel from France to the UK. The Channel, though much narrower than the Mediterranean, is one of the busiest and most hazardous shipping lanes in the world, posing significant dangers to those desperate enough to attempt the journey. For migrants who have endured treacherous overland routes and exploitation at the hands of traffickers, the crossing of the Channel is often the final step in their long and perilous quest for refuge in the UK. Yet, like the Mediterranean, the Channel has become a deadly passage, where the risks are high and the outcomes frequently tragic.

The English Channel: A Deadly and Dangerous Passage

The Channel, while only 21 miles wide at its narrowest point, is a formidable body of water. Strong currents, unpredictable weather, and heavy shipping traffic make it a treacherous stretch, particularly for those attempting to cross in small, overcrowded boats. The vessels used by traffickers are often woefully inadequate for the journey. Inflatable dinghies, typically designed for short trips in calm waters, are overloaded with men, women, and children, making them highly unstable and prone to capsizing. These boats are frequently unfit to handle the rough seas, where strong winds and choppy waters can easily overturn them.

Migrants attempting the crossing often do so at night, to evade detection by French and UK authorities. However, this only adds to the danger, as navigating in the dark on such precarious boats increases the risk of collision with large cargo ships that pass through the Channel at all hours. The Channel's dense traffic, with hundreds of vessels traversing the waters daily, presents a constant threat to small, nearly invisible boats carrying migrants. It is not uncommon for these dinghies to be swamped by the wake of larger vessels or for collisions to occur, leading to fatalities.

Even when the weather is relatively calm, the physical toll of the journey is immense. Many migrants have already suffered malnutrition, dehydration, and physical exhaustion during their arduous trek across Europe. By the time they reach the shores of France, they are often in poor health and ill-prepared for the crossing. Hypothermia is a common risk, as the cold waters of the Channel can rapidly sap the body's heat. Those who fall overboard whether due to capsizing or being knocked into the water by the overcrowded conditions face almost certain death if not rescued immediately, as survival times in the freezing waters are measured in minutes.

Traffickers Exploiting the Channel

Human traffickers, who control much of the illicit movement across the Channel, exploit the desperation of migrants seeking a better life in the UK. Smugglers charge exorbitant fees, often in the thousands of pounds, for a spot on these flimsy boats, promising safe passage and swift arrival on British shores. The traffickers care little for the lives of those they are smuggling. Many migrants are left to navigate the treacherous waters with little to no assistance; they are handed life jackets of questionable quality, given no navigational equipment, and left to the mercy of the sea.

As in Libya and the Mediterranean, traffickers often subject migrants to further exploitation before they even set foot in a boat. Migrants stranded in makeshift camps around Calais and Dunkirk, for example, are regularly forced to live in squalid conditions, preyed upon by criminal gangs and unscrupulous smugglers. The camps, which have been dismantled and rebuilt several times over the years, have become breeding grounds for exploitation, where traffickers extort money from migrants, sometimes demanding additional payments even after promising safe passage. For many, these camps represent a purgatory of sorts trapped in a foreign land, unable to move forward or go back, with traffickers exploiting their desperation at every turn.

The smuggling networks that operate in northern France are sophisticated and constantly shifting their tactics to evade law enforcement. French authorities have worked in cooperation with the UK to crack down on trafficking operations, but the vastness of the coastline and the relentless demand from migrants make it nearly impossible to stem the tide. Traffickers have adapted by launching boats from increasingly remote areas along the coast, making it harder for law enforcement to intercept them before they set off.

The Role of Technology and Law Enforcement

Unlike in the Mediterranean, where EU naval patrols are spread thin across a much larger body of water, the English Channel is more tightly monitored by both French and UK authorities. Drones, radar systems, and patrol boats from both countries attempt to intercept migrant vessels before they reach UK waters. Despite these efforts, the sheer number of crossings has overwhelmed authorities, and many boats slip through undetected. When boats are intercepted, migrants are often returned to France or taken to processing centres in the UK, but traffickers quickly regroup, and the cycle begins again.

In recent years, the number of crossings has increased dramatically, spurred in part by the belief among migrants that the UK offers more favourable asylum conditions and economic opportunities than other European nations. The impact of Brexit, too, has played a role, as the perception that border controls have been weakened has led many to see this as their last chance to reach the UK before regulations tighten further. This influx has strained relations between the UK and France, as both countries grapple with the political, social, and logistical challenges of managing the flow of migrants.

A Political and Humanitarian Crisis

The increasing frequency of crossings has sparked political controversy in the UK, where the government has vowed to take tougher measures to stop illegal immigration. However, these measures, including plans to deport illegal migrants to third countries, have been met with legal challenges and widespread criticism from human rights organisations. Critics argue that such policies fail to address the root causes of migration and trafficking, and instead punish the victims of traffickers.

The humanitarian dimension of this crisis is profound. Many of the people attempting to cross the Channel have fled conflict, persecution, or extreme poverty in their home countries. They have endured long and dangerous journeys across multiple borders, facing exploitation at every stage. By the time they reach northern France, many see the crossing of the Channel not just as their final hurdle but as their only hope of a future free from violence and deprivation. The desperation of these individuals is palpable, and it is this desperation that traffickers exploit so ruthlessly.

For the families left behind when these crossings end in tragedy, the English Channel has become a graveyard. Like the Mediterranean, the Channel is increasingly associated with death and despair, as migrants continue to risk their lives in the hope of reaching safety. Each year, the number of recorded deaths rises, yet the crossings persist, driven by the same combination of desperation, exploitation, and the failure of international systems to offer adequate legal pathways for migration.

A Crisis of Exploitation and Survival

The English Channel, once a symbol of separation and protection for the UK, has now become a symbol of the human cost of migration and trafficking. The perilous crossings mirror the dangers of the Mediterranean, where lives are lost, and families torn apart. The small stretch of water separating France from the UK has become a deadly obstacle for migrants, many of whom have already endured untold suffering.

Traffickers and smugglers, emboldened by the chaos in northern France and the lack of viable migration routes, continue to profit from this misery. The risks to life are immense, yet the promise of safety in the UK keeps driving people to take these extraordinary risks. Like the Mediterranean, the English Channel is a reminder of the broader failures in migration policy, law enforcement, and international cooperation. Until these underlying issues are addressed, the Channel will remain a deadly crossing, where human traffickers thrive and where too many lives are lost in pursuit of hope.

Air Routes: False Promises and Legal Loopholes

Though less physically dangerous than land or sea routes, air routes used by traffickers are no less insidious. These methods often involve deception, with traffickers using legitimate airlines to transport victims under the guise of employment, education, or even marriage. Victims may be issued fraudulent visas or be coerced into travelling on temporary work permits, only to find themselves enslaved upon arrival.

Traffickers exploit the legal complexities of international air travel to move their victims, taking advantage of inconsistent visa regimes and lax oversight at some airports. The wealthier nations of the Gulf, for instance, are notorious for the exploitation of migrant domestic workers, many of whom are trafficked from South Asia under false promises of employment. These air routes often start in countries like India, Pakistan, and the Philippines, with traffickers forging documents or bribing officials to facilitate their travel.

In the context of the West, victims are sometimes trafficked into the USA, Canada, or the UK through similar air routes. Traffickers recruit victims with offers of domestic work, au pair positions, or jobs in the hospitality industry, only to subject them to forced labour or sexual exploitation upon their arrival. The air routes are favoured because they allow traffickers to evade the harsher conditions and risks associated with land and sea routes, although they often rely on corrupt networks that span both the source and destination countries.

The trafficking of illegal migrants into the USA has taken on increasingly sophisticated forms in recent years, particularly using air routes that provide an appearance of legality while masking a deeper, more troubling reality. Under the current Biden-Harris administration, various immigration programs and policies have contributed to an influx of migrants, some of whom are transported via air routes and then released into the country with minimal oversight. This lack of stringent checks has allowed traffickers to take advantage of the system, often preying on the most vulnerable women, children, and unaccompanied minors. The disturbing reality is that many of these migrants, once within US borders, fall into the hands of trafficking networks, with missing children being one of the most alarming consequences of this flawed process.

A New Avenue for Trafficking

While much attention has been focused on the US-Mexico land border and the dangerous journeys many migrants undertake on foot or by vehicle, air routes have quietly become another means by which illegal migrants enter the country. Under certain immigration programs, migrants are flown directly into the United States, bypassing the harsh conditions of overland smuggling but not necessarily escaping the grip of trafficking networks. This has largely gone under the radar, as air travel presents a veneer of legality and order, but it has become yet another channel through which traffickers operate with relative impunity.

One of the ways this happens is through government-sponsored or NGO-facilitated flights that transport migrants from Latin America or other regions to various cities across the US. These programs are often framed as humanitarian efforts or responses to asylum claims. However, there is growing concern that once these individuals arrive in the United States, many are released with little to no follow-up. With lax oversight, particularly for minors, these migrants are vulnerable to exploitation by traffickers waiting on the other side.

The fact that air travel allows migrants to avoid the physical dangers of crossing the desert or scaling border fences does not mean they are safe. The danger simply shifts from the physical to the psychological and legal realm. For children and unaccompanied minors, the risks are particularly high. Upon arriving in the United States, many of these children are placed into the custody of sponsors, some of whom may have ties to trafficking networks. The process for vetting these sponsors has been criticised as being too lax, with cases emerging of children being handed over to individuals who then exploit or traffic them. In many cases, these children simply disappear, becoming part of the disturbing statistic of "missing children" who vanished after entering the country.

The Role of Government Policies

Under the Biden-Harris administration, policies that have sought to manage the immigration crisis at the border have intentionally opened up avenues for traffickers to exploit. Programs such as *Title 42*, initially implemented during the Trump administration to rapidly expel migrants due to public health concerns, have been selectively applied or lifted, creating confusion and opportunities for traffickers to manipulate the system. Moreover, the administration has implemented policies that allow certain categories of migrants, particularly families and unaccompanied minors, to be flown into the United States under the guise of humanitarian protection or asylum.

For example, the *Unaccompanied Alien Children (UAC)* program, designed to offer protection to minors arriving without parents, has faced significant scrutiny. Under this program, unaccompanied minors are flown into the United States and placed with sponsors or in temporary housing. However, the sponsors are often not thoroughly vetted, and there have been numerous reports of children being handed over to traffickers or individuals who exploit them for forced labour, sexual slavery, or other illicit purposes. The Office of Refugee Resettlement, tasked with overseeing the placement of these children, has been overwhelmed by the sheer number of cases, leading to gaps in oversight that traffickers eagerly exploit.

What compounds the issue is the growing backlog in immigration courts, which means that many of these migrants, including minors, are released with court dates years into the future. In the interim, they are left to fend for themselves in a country where traffickers are well-organised and have networks in place to recruit, exploit, and abuse them. The lack of adequate follow-up and the overwhelming strain on social services mean that these children often fall through the cracks, making them prime targets for trafficking networks.

The Trafficking of Missing Children

One of the most alarming aspects of this situation is the fate of children who arrive in the United States through these air routes and then disappear. Many unaccompanied minors who are flown into the country are eventually reported as "missing," with no trace of their whereabouts after being placed with sponsors. These children are particularly vulnerable to human traffickers, who can easily exploit the gaps in the system to abduct them and force them into exploitative situations.

The trafficking of children in the United States is not a new problem, but the current immigration policies have exacerbated it. Once in the hands of traffickers, these children are often forced into labour, coerced into the sex trade, or otherwise exploited in underground markets. Because many of these children arrive without proper identification or family connections, it is difficult for authorities to track them once they vanish. The traffickers who exploit these children know how to manipulate the system, using fake documents and shifting them between different locations to avoid detection.

The problem has reached such a scale that even government officials have admitted that they have lost track of thousands of children who have arrived in the country under these programs. The Health and Human Services (HHS) department, responsible for placing unaccompanied minors with sponsors, has come under fire for its inability to follow up on the welfare of these children once they are released. Investigations have revealed that many of these children are placed in unsafe conditions, with some falling victim to trafficking rings operating across state lines.

Exploiting the Air Routes

Trafficking networks have become increasingly adept at exploiting the opportunities presented by air travel. Rather than relying solely on the dangerous and highly monitored land routes, traffickers use air routes to bring migrants, including minors, into the United States under the radar. In some cases, traffickers pose as relatives or legitimate sponsors to gain custody of children arriving through the UAC program or other humanitarian initiatives. Once these children are in their custody, they are moved across state lines, disappearing into the network of forced labour, prostitution, or servitude.

Furthermore, some traffickers have infiltrated the very systems designed to protect vulnerable migrants. Investigations have uncovered cases where individuals posing as aid workers or legal sponsors have been involved in trafficking operations. They use their positions to gain the trust of authorities, secure the release of children, and then traffic them within the United States. This chilling reality underscores the need for much more rigorous vetting and follow-up in the placement of unaccompanied minors, as well as closer cooperation between immigration authorities and anti-trafficking agencies.

The Need for Reform

The current situation demands urgent attention and reform. The use of air routes to transport migrants into the United States is not inherently problematic, but the lack of adequate safeguards, oversight, and follow-up has made it a fertile ground for traffickers to exploit. The Biden-Harris administration's immigration policies have created an environment where traffickers can thrive.

Addressing this issue requires a multi-faceted approach. First, there must be stricter vetting processes for sponsors, particularly those taking custody of unaccompanied minors. The current system, which relies heavily on self-reported information and minimal background checks, is insufficient. A more thorough vetting process, combined with regular check-ins on the welfare of these children, is essential to prevent them from falling into the hands of traffickers.

Secondly, there needs to be better interagency coordination between immigration authorities, law enforcement, and anti-trafficking units. Trafficking networks operate across borders and state lines and combating them requires a unified approach that spans both domestic and international agencies. Immigration courts, refugee resettlement agencies, and child protective services must work together more effectively to ensure that vulnerable migrants, particularly children, are not lost in the system.

Finally, there must be a recognition that the root causes of trafficking and exploitation poverty, conflict, and instability in migrants' home countries and the draw of free medical and social benefits must be addressed if the flow of trafficked individuals is to be stemmed. Without a holistic approach that addresses both the demand for trafficked labour and the vulnerabilities that drive people into the hands of traffickers, these air routes will continue to be exploited, and the crisis will persist.

As such, the trafficking of illegal migrants into the United States via air routes has become a dark and disturbing reality under the current administration. While purported to offer humanitarian aid, these programs have been co-opted by traffickers who prey on the most vulnerable, particularly children. The increasing number of missing children, many of whom fall into the hands of traffickers, underscores the urgency of reforming the system. Without stronger safeguards and better oversight, these air routes will continue to serve as conduits for human trafficking, further perpetuating the cycle of exploitation and suffering.

Shifting Routes and Evasive Tactics

One of the greatest challenges in combating trafficking is that the routes used by traffickers are constantly shifting. As law enforcement agencies clamp down on known hot spots, traffickers adapt by seeking new, less monitored routes. The closure of certain land or sea pathways may result in the opening of others; for example, when Greek authorities increased border patrols in the Aegean, traffickers began to divert their victims through more remote parts of the Mediterranean, or alternative land routes via the Balkans.

In the Americas, increased enforcement at the US-Mexico border has not deterred trafficking but has instead forced traffickers to use more sophisticated methods, such as tunnels or even drones to transport contraband. These changes reflect the fluid nature of trafficking networks, which evolve in response to both enforcement and geopolitical events, such as the war in Syria or the economic collapse in Venezuela.

Conclusion

As we have seen, the routes to exploitation are as varied and complex as the criminal networks that manage them. From the dangerous crossings at the US-Mexico border to the perilous journeys across the Mediterranean, and the deceptive use of air travel, traffickers constantly shift their tactics to evade law enforcement. In each of these regions, a combination of poverty, corruption, conflict, and inadequate legal frameworks allows traffickers to thrive, preying on the vulnerable with brutal efficiency. Understanding these routes and how they function is essential if we are to devise effective strategies to combat trafficking in the West.

In the next chapter, I will delve deeper into the recruitment methods traffickers use, examining how vulnerable individuals are targeted, manipulated, and coerced into exploitation, further perpetuating this global crisis. This analysis will be critical to understanding how the seemingly distant crisis of trafficking reaches into the very heart of Western societies.

Chapter 3: Profiles of the Victims: Who Are They?

In the labyrinth of human trafficking, victims come from diverse backgrounds, spanning continents and cultures, yet they share common threads of vulnerability. Trafficking thrives on exploitation, preying on the most defenceless those who are already marginalised by poverty, war, or societal exclusion. These individuals are not just nameless faces in a sea of statistics; they are people with families, aspirations, and futures tragically hijacked by a merciless underground industry.

Women and Girls: The Faces Behind the Tragedy

Women and girls make up a disproportionate share of trafficking victims worldwide, and sexual exploitation remains the most brutal form of abuse they endure. This gendered aspect of human trafficking is not incidental but deeply rooted in long-standing socio-economic inequalities, cultural biases, and global poverty patterns that place women at particular risk. Traffickers, aware of the hardships these women face, systematically exploit their vulnerabilities, promising them opportunities that seem like a lifeline. Whether it's the offer of employment, education, or marriage, traffickers manipulate the hopes and aspirations of these women, preying on their desire to escape their harsh realities. Yet, the promises they receive are mere facades, hiding the grim reality of forced prostitution, sexual slavery, and unrelenting abuse.

Vulnerable Groups and the Global Reach of Trafficking

Women from specific regions are particularly vulnerable due to a combination of economic desperation, political instability, and entrenched gender inequalities. Eastern Europe, with its long-standing socio-economic struggles in the post-Soviet era, has become one of the primary regions from which traffickers source victims. Countries like Ukraine, Moldova, and Romania, where poverty is widespread and social safety nets are fragile, are frequent hunting grounds for traffickers. Southeast Asia, with nations like Thailand, the Philippines, and Vietnam, is another region where poverty and limited employment opportunities drive many women into the arms of traffickers. In parts of sub-Saharan Africa, such as Nigeria, traffickers exploit social and economic desperation, often operating with impunity due to weak governance and widespread corruption.

In some particularly harrowing cases, these women are sold by their own families. Driven by desperate financial circumstances, families in impoverished regions may be misled by traffickers posing as employment brokers, believing that sending their daughters abroad is the only way to ensure their future prosperity. These families may be told that their daughters will find work as housekeepers, and waitresses, or even receive an education, with promises of remittances that will help lift them out of poverty. Instead, these women are coerced into prostitution or other forms of sexual servitude, with the traffickers extracting profits from their exploitation.

Once trapped in this vicious cycle, victims are often moved across borders, making it harder for authorities to trace their whereabouts or for the victims themselves to seek help. As we explored in Chapter 2, traffickers are adept at shifting their routes to avoid detection, and the transnational nature of these criminal networks makes it challenging for law enforcement agencies to track down and rescue victims. Women and girls may be passed through multiple hands, sold from one trafficker to another, until they are completely lost within the system.

This profile of female victims varies considerably across different regions, as cultural, economic, and political factors shape their vulnerabilities in unique ways. In the following sections, I will explore the backgrounds of women trafficked from various parts of the world, illustrating the distinct risks they face and the common threads that unite their tragic stories.

Eastern European Women: Betrayed by the Dream of a Better Life

For many women from Eastern Europe, particularly from countries like Ukraine, Moldova, Romania, and Bulgaria, the post-Soviet era has been marked by significant economic upheaval. The collapse of the Soviet Union left many of these countries in financial ruin, with high unemployment rates and scant social support systems. As a result, women from these regions often find themselves trapped in cycles of poverty, with limited opportunities for education or employment.

Traffickers take advantage of this economic desperation. They frequently present themselves as recruiters for legitimate jobs, offering positions as waitresses, nannies, or domestic workers in wealthier European nations. In many cases, these traffickers are local and appear trustworthy, often promising attractive salaries and the chance to send money home to struggling families. In some instances, traffickers even prey on the ambitions of young women by posing as modelling agents, promising careers that will lift them out of poverty.

Once lured by these promises, the reality is starkly different. These women are trafficked across borders, their passports confiscated upon arrival, and are often forced into prostitution. Many are moved between countries in Western Europe, making it difficult for law enforcement to track their movements. Others are sold between different traffickers, treated as commodities in a market that values them solely for the profits their bodies can generate.

A notable example is the high number of Romanian women trafficked into Western Europe, particularly Italy and Spain, where they are coerced into prostitution rings. Often, they are held in debt bondage, forced to work to pay off fictional "debts" that grow endlessly, ensuring that they remain trapped in servitude. In some cases, these women are threatened with violence or told that harm will come to their families back home if they attempt to escape.

The allure of the West, with its promise of financial security and upward mobility, continues to draw many women from Eastern Europe into the web of traffickers. The contrast between the dream of a better life and the horrific reality they encounter is a testament to the emotional and psychological manipulation employed by traffickers, who understand the deep-seated desperation of these women.

Southeast Asian Women: Exploited by False Promises of Work

In Southeast Asia, countries like Thailand, the Philippines, Vietnam, and Cambodia are major sources of trafficked women. Here, the socio-economic factors driving trafficking are similar to those in Eastern Europe, but with the added complexity of rural poverty and deeply ingrained gender inequalities. In many rural areas of Southeast Asia, young women face the expectation of providing for their families, and the pressure to send money home can be overwhelming. With few viable employment options locally, these women become prime targets for traffickers.

Many of these women are lured by the promise of work in major urban centres or abroad, particularly in wealthier Asian nations like Malaysia, and Singapore, and even as far afield as the Middle East. Domestic work is one of the most common pretexts under which women from Southeast Asia are trafficked. Traffickers, posing as recruitment agents, promise employment as maids, caregivers, or factory workers. The promise of a steady income in foreign currency is an attractive proposition for women who see no other means of supporting their families.

However, upon arrival, these women often find themselves in situations of sexual exploitation, forced to work in brothels or massage parlours. In Thailand, for instance, there is a thriving sex tourism industry that fuels the demand for trafficked women, not only from Thailand itself but also from neighbouring countries like Laos, Myanmar, and Cambodia. The women are held in captivity, their passports taken away, and their movements strictly controlled. They are forced to work long hours under threat of violence, often in appalling conditions, and they are rarely paid the wages they were promised.

The shame associated with sex work, particularly in conservative Southeast Asian cultures, also serves as a powerful tool for traffickers to control their victims. Women are often told that if they try to escape, their families will be informed of their "shameful" activities, or worse, they will be ostracised upon returning home. In some cases, traffickers even use religion to further manipulate their victims, convincing them that their suffering is a form of penance or punishment for past wrongdoings.

African Women: Trafficked through Organised Networks

The trafficking of women from sub-Saharan Africa, particularly Nigeria, is one of the most documented and complex cases of human trafficking. Nigerian women, in particular, are trafficked in large numbers to Europe, especially Italy, where they are forced into prostitution. This trafficking is often organised by powerful crime syndicates that operate across borders, involving a network of recruiters, transporters, and enforcers who ensure that victims remain under their control at all times.

Many Nigerian women come from regions plagued by poverty, political instability, and corruption. In particular, the Edo State in southern Nigeria has become notorious as a major source of trafficked women. These women are often promised work in Europe as cleaners or domestic workers. Some are even deceived into believing they will be studying or entering into legitimate employment contracts. However, the reality they face once they arrive in Europe is entirely different.

Traffickers use elaborate rituals and oaths, known as "juju," to psychologically bind these women into compliance. The juju rituals, performed before the women depart Nigeria, involve blood oaths and threats of spiritual retribution should they disobey their traffickers or try to escape. Many victims firmly believe that breaking their oath will result in severe harm to themselves or their families. This psychological manipulation, combined with physical violence, ensures that the women remain in the traffickers' control, even when they are hundreds of miles from home.

In Europe, Nigerian women are often forced to work in street prostitution, particularly in Italy, where they are subjected to brutal working conditions. They are frequently moved from one city to another, making it difficult for authorities to track them or for the women to establish any sense of stability. Many of them are trapped in a cycle of debt bondage, where they are forced to pay off exorbitant amounts of money supposedly owed for their travel to Europe. As with other trafficked women, the promise of freedom remains tantalisingly out of reach as the "debt" continues to grow with every passing day.

South and Central American Women: Lured by the American Dream

In Latin America, the trafficking of women, particularly from countries like Venezuela, Colombia, and Honduras, is a growing issue. Women from these regions are often fleeing gang violence, political instability, or economic collapse, and the promise of work in the United States or other wealthy nations is a powerful draw. Much like their counterparts from other regions, these women are often recruited by traffickers posing as legitimate employment agents, offering jobs in housekeeping, agriculture, or even the hospitality industry.

Venezuelan women, in particular, have been increasingly trafficked due to the country's ongoing economic crisis, which has left millions in poverty and created a mass exodus of refugees. Traffickers exploit the vulnerability of these women, who are desperate to escape the dire conditions at home. Once lured into trafficking networks, many are smuggled through dangerous land routes, often passing through Mexico on their way to the United States. The journey itself is perilous, with women subjected to sexual violence at the hands of traffickers, smugglers, or even law enforcement officials along the way.

Upon reaching their destination, these women often find themselves forced into sex work or unpaid domestic labour. The allure of the "American Dream" becomes a distant memory as they are trapped in a cycle of exploitation and abuse. In some cases, trafficked women from Latin America are coerced into working in illegal brothels or sweatshops, hidden in plain sight in major American cities.

The Complex Web of Vulnerabilities

What unites these diverse profiles of women trafficked from Eastern Europe, Southeast Asia, Africa, and Latin America is their vulnerability. Traffickers exploit economic desperation, cultural pressures, and false promises to ensnare these women in a web of exploitation that spans the globe. Whether lured by the promise of work, education, or a new life, these women are deceived into entering a system that profits from their suffering.

The dream of a better life in Europe, North America, or other wealthy regions is a potent motivator for many women, particularly those from countries where opportunities are scarce, and social mobility is virtually non-existent. The idea of escaping poverty or escaping conflict common in parts of Africa, Southeast Asia, and Eastern Europe makes these women easy targets for traffickers. In many cases, the traffickers present themselves as employment agents, modelling scouts, or even prospective spouses, offering what appears to be a legitimate chance to start anew.

In reality, these hopeful journeys quickly turn into nightmarish experiences. Women are deceived and coerced into a life of forced prostitution, sexual slavery, or other forms of sexual exploitation, often under horrendous conditions. The psychological toll is enormous, as these women are not only physically abused but also subjected to repeated mental manipulation, creating an environment in which they feel isolated, powerless, and incapable of escape.

The Mechanisms of Control

Traffickers use a variety of tactics to maintain control over their victims. One of the most common strategies is to confiscate passports and identification documents upon arrival, leaving the women without any legal identity. This not only makes it nearly impossible for them to seek help but also increases their fear of deportation or imprisonment if they are discovered by authorities in a foreign country. By keeping them undocumented, traffickers ensure that their victims remain dependent and isolated, often in environments where they do not speak the language and have no social network to rely on.

Physical violence and threats of harm are also frequently employed to keep women in line. Many trafficked women are beaten, raped, and subjected to other forms of brutal physical abuse. Beyond the immediate violence, traffickers often use threats of harm against their families back home as an additional form of psychological coercion. This creates a deep sense of helplessness in the victims, as they feel trapped not only by their circumstances but also by the potential danger posed to their loved ones. Even when they are not physically restrained, the combination of fear, psychological manipulation, and cultural isolation ensures that most victims feel they have no choice but to comply.

Sexual slavery and exploitation also often come with forced drug addiction. In some cases, traffickers deliberately get their victims addicted to substances such as heroin or methamphetamines, further tightening their control. The combination of dependency on drugs and the trauma of repeated sexual exploitation creates a situation where victims are less likely to seek escape, as their mental and physical health deteriorates rapidly.

Global Demand for Exploited Women

It is important to recognise that this exploitation is driven by a global demand for trafficked women, particularly in the West. The prostitution industry in Western nations, while often hidden from mainstream society, is a major destination for women trafficked from poorer regions of the world. The demand for cheap, illegal sex work provides traffickers with lucrative incentives, as the profits from exploiting these women far outweigh the risks of being caught. This dark market operates across major cities in Europe and North America, feeding off the anonymity and mobility that modern urban environments provide.

Additionally, in many Western nations, legal frameworks meant to combat trafficking are often undermined by the social stigma that surrounds sex work. Victims of trafficking, particularly those involved in prostitution, are often criminalised rather than seen as individuals in need of help. The fear of being prosecuted, coupled with a lack of access to proper legal representation or social services, leaves many victims feeling that escape is impossible. In this way, the social and legal environment of many Western countries indirectly perpetuates the suffering of trafficked women by failing to provide them with safe avenues for recovery and justice.

The Long-Term Consequences for Victims

For those who do manage to escape, the trauma of their experiences can be long-lasting. Many victims suffer from post-traumatic stress disorder (PTSD), depression, and anxiety, as well as physical health issues resulting from years of abuse. The stigma attached to being a trafficking victim, especially for those involved in sex work, often makes reintegration into society difficult. Women who have been trafficked are often treated as social outcasts, and in some cases, their families may reject them, believing that they have disgraced their households.

Even in countries where support services exist, the path to recovery is fraught with challenges. Psychological scars, coupled with a lack of formal education or professional skills, make it difficult for survivors to rebuild their lives. The cycle of exploitation and abuse, which often begins with poverty and desperation, may tragically continue even after they have escaped the clutches of traffickers. Many trafficked women end up living in precarious conditions, with few opportunities to create a stable, fulfilling life.

Conclusion

The trafficking of women and girls for sexual exploitation is one of the most pervasive and damaging forms of modern slavery. These victims, drawn from some of the most vulnerable populations around the world, are subjected to unimaginable horrors, driven by global demand for illicit sex work and perpetuated by criminal networks that span continents. By examining who these victims are, where they come from, and how they are exploited, we can begin to understand the magnitude of the human suffering involved and the urgent need for international action to combat this heinous trade.

Understanding their profiles and the mechanisms of their exploitation, as we have seen in this chapter, provides a foundation for addressing the broader systemic issues that allow trafficking to flourish. Only through a concerted effort at both the local and global levels can we hope to dismantle the trafficking networks that continue to prey on women and girls, and provide survivors with the support and resources they need to heal.

Traffickers use deceitful recruitment strategies, often operating under the guise of legitimate employment agencies or modelling scouts. Upon arrival in the West, these women are stripped of their identification, rendered voiceless in unfamiliar environments, and coerced into submission through violence or threats against their loved ones back home. Many are smuggled through the same routes discussed in Chapter 2, entering the West illegally, which only increases their fear of deportation or imprisonment if they seek help.

The exploitation doesn't end with forced sex work. These women are often treated as disposable commodities traded, sold, and moved across borders with little regard for their humanity. In some Western countries, even though there are laws designed to help victims, the stigma associated with sex work traps them in a cycle of shame and fear, making escape nearly impossible.

Children: Stolen Innocence and Exploited Labour

Children represent one of the most heart-wrenching categories of trafficking victims. From the streets of Southeast Asia to the rural farmlands of Latin America, children are frequently targeted by traffickers for both sexual exploitation and forced labour. Their vulnerability, innocence, and lack of resources make them easy prey for those looking to exploit their bodies or labour for profit. Across the globe, children are trafficked across borders, often from impoverished, conflict-ridden regions where law enforcement and social services are either overwhelmed or non-existent. In many cases, these children come from families who have been deceived into believing that their offspring will receive education or job opportunities abroad. Instead, they are thrust into unimaginable circumstances sold into prostitution, forced into domestic servitude, or made to toil in fields and factories under inhumane conditions.

Trafficked for Sexual Exploitation: The Innocence Stolen

The trafficking of children for sexual exploitation is one of the most egregious violations of human rights, with devastating psychological and physical consequences for the victims. Traffickers target vulnerable children, especially girls, although boys are not immune, promising them a future that quickly turns into a nightmare. In Southeast Asia, for instance, countries like Thailand and Cambodia have long been hubs for the commercial sexual exploitation of children, with demand driven by both domestic and foreign clientele, including sex tourists. Traffickers lure children from rural areas or impoverished families, often through promises of education or work in urban centres. Instead, these children are funnelled into brothels or forced into street prostitution.

In Latin America, countries like Brazil, Honduras, and Mexico face similar issues, where children, particularly young girls, are targeted by traffickers for prostitution rings. The trafficking of children in these regions is often tied to organised crime, and it is not uncommon for trafficked girls to be controlled through threats of violence or even death. Some children are kidnapped outright, while others are sold by their own families that, out of desperation or ignorance, believe they are providing their children with a better future. The pervasive poverty and lack of educational opportunities make it easy for traffickers to convince parents that sending their child abroad or to a city will result in legitimate work. But the children instead face unimaginable horrors, becoming mere commodities in a brutal underground market.

Children as Labourers: Hidden Behind the Supply Chains

While sexual exploitation is the most publicised form of child trafficking, forced labour is equally devastating, and it often receives far less attention. Children trafficked for labour are forced to work in dangerous, exploitative conditions whether in illegal sweatshops, mining operations, or agricultural fields. These children are subjected to gruelling work, long hours, and often no pay, working in environments that deprive them of both safety and dignity.

In regions such as West Africa, child labour in the cocoa industry has been a significant issue for decades. Many children, some as young as five or six years old, are trafficked from countries like Mali and Burkina Faso to work on cocoa plantations in Côte d'Ivoire and Ghana. These children are forced to perform physically demanding tasks, such as harvesting cocoa beans or applying pesticides, with no protection or compensation. They live in deplorable conditions, deprived of education and necessities, and they are often beaten or subjected to severe punishment if they fail to meet the traffickers' demands. Despite international efforts to end child labour in this industry, the problem persists, largely because the children involved are hidden within complex supply chains that obscure the exploitation of end consumers.

A similar situation exists in Southeast Asia, where children are trafficked to work in the fishing industry. Boys, in particular, are forced to work long hours on fishing boats, often in unsafe conditions, where they are subjected to physical abuse and denied wages. Many are kept at sea for months or even years, effectively becoming slaves to their traffickers. The seafood industry, like many other global supply chains, often masks the origins of products, making it difficult for authorities or consumers to trace the exploitation of children.

Refugee Children: Lost in the Chaos of Migration

Refugee children, separated from their families during migration or displaced by conflict, are particularly susceptible to trafficking. As discussed in Chapter 1, the global displacement crisis, fuelled by wars in Syria, Afghanistan, and other regions, has created a fertile breeding ground for traffickers to operate with impunity. The chaos that accompanies large-scale migration, especially in conflict zones, leaves children highly vulnerable to exploitation. Many of these children are undocumented, living on the fringes of society, and as such, they are almost invisible to authorities. This lack of documentation combined with weak border controls and overwhelmed international agencies makes it easy for traffickers to target refugee children without fear of detection.

Traffickers often pose as aid workers or trusted adults, offering assistance to refugee children who have been separated from their families. In some cases, traffickers will infiltrate refugee camps, where unaccompanied children are particularly vulnerable. These children are then smuggled across borders and exploited for both sexual and labour purposes. In Europe, the refugee crisis has led to a surge in the number of unaccompanied minors arriving from countries like Syria, Iraq, and Afghanistan. These children, who have often experienced the trauma of war and displacement, are ripe targets for traffickers. Many are forced into prostitution or used as forced labour in industries ranging from agriculture to construction.

In the United States, a similar dynamic is playing out at the southern border, where unaccompanied minors from Central America fleeing gang violence and economic desperation are often intercepted by traffickers. These children, already traumatised by their journeys, are manipulated into situations of exploitation. Some are forced to work in agricultural fields or sweatshops, while others are coerced into sex work. The sheer number of children crossing borders without documentation or adult supervision makes it difficult for authorities to track their whereabouts, providing traffickers with the perfect opportunity to exploit them.

The Complexities of Domestic Servitude

Another insidious form of child trafficking is domestic servitude, where children, often girls, are forced to work as domestic help in private households. This form of trafficking is particularly common in regions such as Southeast Asia, West Africa, and parts of Latin America. Children are often trafficked under the guise of "apprenticeships" or "household training," where families are convinced that their child will learn valuable skills in a foreign country or major city. Instead, these children are forced into servitude, cooking, cleaning, and performing other household tasks for little or no pay.

In many cases, these children live with their employers, where they are subjected to physical and emotional abuse. They are often isolated from the outside world, making it difficult for them to seek help or escape. Domestic servitude is a particularly challenging form of trafficking to combat because it occurs behind closed doors, out of the public eye, and is often accepted as a normal practice in certain cultures. In some regions, the use of child servants is culturally ingrained, making it difficult to distinguish between legitimate apprenticeships and cases of trafficking.

Children and Organ Trafficking: A Hidden Horror

A lesser-known but equally horrific form of child trafficking involves organ harvesting. In certain parts of the world, particularly in regions plagued by corruption and weak governance, children are trafficked for the explicit purpose of having their organs harvested and sold on the black market. This gruesome trade is driven by the high demand for organs in both developed and developing nations, where patients with life-threatening illnesses are willing to pay exorbitant sums for transplants.

Children, especially those who are unregistered or undocumented, are particularly vulnerable to this form of trafficking. Traffickers often target homeless children, orphans, or refugees those whose disappearances are less likely to be noticed. Once trafficked, these children may be killed for their organs, which are then sold to unscrupulous doctors or medical facilities. This dark and hidden side of trafficking is particularly difficult to combat, as it operates within highly clandestine networks that are difficult to penetrate.

The Invisible Suffering of Trafficked Children

The trafficking of children, whether for sexual exploitation, forced labour, domestic servitude, or organ harvesting, represents one of the most severe humanitarian crises of our time. These children are often invisible, unseen by the authorities, forgotten by society, and trapped in a cycle of exploitation from which they cannot escape. Whether they are lured by false promises of education and work or kidnapped outright, their stories are united by the overwhelming sense of betrayal and loss that defines their young lives.

As we look for solutions, international agencies, governments, and civil society must work together to provide better protection for children, particularly those most vulnerable to trafficking. This includes improving documentation and monitoring systems for displaced and migrant children, increasing awareness in source countries, and holding industries accountable for exploitative labour practices. Until these efforts are fully realised, the invisible suffering of trafficked children will continue to plague our world, hidden in the shadows but no less devastating.

Men: Forced Labour and Economic Exploitation

While the plight of women and children often dominates discussions on human trafficking, it is crucial to recognise that men too are significant victims of this global atrocity, particularly in the realm of forced labour. The trafficking of men is a pervasive issue that often operates under the radar, overshadowed by the more visible forms of exploitation involving women and children. These men, primarily migrant workers from impoverished regions, are lured with promises of employment, only to find themselves trapped in exploitative, dangerous, and degrading conditions.

The Lure of Prosperity: False Promises and Harsh Realities

For many men from Africa, Asia, and Latin America, the allure of a better life abroad is powerful. Faced with economic despair, political instability, or violent conflict, these men see migration as a pathway to security and prosperity. They are promised legitimate jobs in construction, agriculture, manufacturing, or hospitality sectors that often rely on migrant labour. However, these promises are little more than bait used by traffickers to trap them in a web of exploitation.

In regions such as Southeast Asia, men from countries like Bangladesh, Nepal, and the Philippines are frequently recruited to work in the Gulf States, lured by the prospect of well-paying jobs in construction or domestic service. Similarly, men from Central and South America are often trafficked into the United States or Canada, promised jobs as farm labourers or factory workers. These promises, however, quickly unravel upon their arrival in the destination country. Traffickers confiscate their passports and documents, leaving them undocumented and unable to seek legal recourse. Without official papers, these men are at the mercy of their traffickers, trapped in an endless cycle of labour under conditions that verge on slavery.

Exploitative Conditions: A Life of Labour and Deprivation

Once trafficked, these men find themselves working in gruelling, exploitative environments. Construction sites, factories, agricultural fields, and even fishing vessels become the sites of their suffering. They are forced to endure long hours of back-breaking labour under dangerous and often life-threatening conditions. Safety regulations, where they exist at all, are routinely ignored, and injuries are common. But even more harrowing is the psychological toll trafficked men are subjected to physical abuse, verbal threats, and the constant fear of deportation or violence against their families.

In the Middle East, particularly in countries like Saudi Arabia, Qatar, and the UAE, migrant men from South Asia work under what is often termed the "kafala" system a sponsorship regime that ties workers to their employers, who exert almost total control over their lives. Men working on construction projects, such as the notorious sites built for events like the FIFA World Cup in Qatar, have reported conditions akin to modern slavery. Withholding of wages, confiscation of passports, overcrowded and unsanitary living conditions, and limited access to food and medical care are all common tactics used by traffickers and unscrupulous employers to maintain control over these men.

Similarly, in Western countries, men trafficked into agricultural work or low-wage industries like meatpacking and manufacturing face exploitative working conditions with little to no pay. In the United States, migrant workers from Mexico and Central America, many of whom are trafficked across the southern border, endure long hours picking crops under the blazing sun, often living in squalid conditions without access to proper shelter or sanitation. Wages are frequently withheld or drastically reduced, with traffickers ensuring these men remain dependent on them for necessities. The fact that many of these men are undocumented makes it almost impossible for them to report the abuse, as they fear deportation or retaliation from traffickers.

Migrant Men: Invisible in the System

Much like the women trafficked for sexual exploitation, trafficked men are often invisible to the system. Their undocumented status makes it difficult for them to seek help or assert their rights. Without legal papers, they cannot approach authorities, access social services, or find alternative employment. This vulnerability is compounded by the fact that labour trafficking, unlike sexual trafficking, often occurs in industries that are considered legitimate, making it harder to detect and dismantle.

Many of these trafficked men are employed in informal labour markets such as day labour, seasonal agricultural work, or small-scale manufacturing that operate on the fringes of legality. These industries thrive on cheap, undocumented labour, and traffickers exploit the lack of oversight and regulation to force men into near-slavery conditions. Western economies, particularly in the agricultural and construction sectors, are often unknowingly complicit in this trade. The demand for cheap labour drives traffickers to smuggle men across borders, as discussed in Chapter 2, making labour trafficking a profitable venture with relatively low risk.

For example, in Europe, the demand for agricultural workers in countries like Italy and Spain has led to the trafficking of men from North Africa and Eastern Europe. These men are often forced to work in fields picking fruits and vegetables, enduring long hours for little to no pay. Living in makeshift camps with no access to basic sanitation, they are completely isolated from the outside world, unable to leave or seek help. In the UK, the modern slavery crisis has revealed widespread exploitation of migrant men in industries such as construction and waste management, where traffickers take advantage of lax labour laws and unregulated markets to profit from the men's suffering.

Forced Labour on the High Seas: Trafficking in the Fishing Industry

Another particularly brutal form of labour trafficking involves the exploitation of men in the fishing industry. In Southeast Asia, men from countries such as Myanmar, Cambodia, and the Philippines are trafficked onto fishing vessels, where they are forced to work under conditions that have been described as "floating prisons." These men, many of whom were promised legitimate work in factories or construction, find themselves trapped on fishing boats for months or even years, unable to escape.

The conditions on these boats are horrific. Men are forced to work long hours, often without food or rest, and are subjected to physical abuse if they fail to meet the traffickers' demands. Many report being beaten, whipped, or tortured, and some have witnessed fellow crew members being thrown overboard for disobedience. The isolation of the high seas makes it almost impossible for these men to seek help or escape, and they are often paid nothing for their labour. The seafood industry, much like agriculture, benefits from these invisible victims, as the trafficking of men into the fishing industry is hidden within complex supply chains that obscure the true cost of cheap seafood in Western markets.

The Cycle of Vulnerability: How Men Are Trapped in Trafficking Networks

The trafficking of men is not just a consequence of poverty and migration; it is a reflection of broader socio-economic structures that make certain populations more vulnerable to exploitation. Men from regions affected by political instability, war, and economic collapse are often desperate to leave their countries, and traffickers prey on this desperation. In many cases, trafficked men are aware of the risks but see no other option. They are willing to take the chance because the alternative of staying in their home country without work or prospects is just as grim.

In Africa, for example, men from countries like Nigeria, Ghana, and Sudan are frequently trafficked into Europe, where they are forced to work in construction or agriculture. These men often pay smugglers vast sums of money to be transported across the Mediterranean, only to find themselves in debt bondage, where their traffickers demand additional payments, forcing them to work under brutal conditions to repay their supposed "debts." The lure of Western prosperity is a powerful draw, but once ensnared in trafficking networks, these men are left with no way out.

Addressing the Hidden Exploitation of Trafficked Men

The trafficking of men, particularly for forced labour, is a hidden crisis that demands urgent attention. While much of the global focus on trafficking has rightly been on women and children, the suffering of trafficked men must not be ignored. Men, especially migrant workers, are just as vulnerable to the tactics of traffickers, and they endure appalling exploitation in industries that benefit from their silence and invisibility.

Combatting the trafficking of men requires a multi-faceted approach. Governments must improve labour protections and enforce regulations in industries that rely heavily on migrant workers, particularly in agriculture, construction, and fishing. Additionally, there must be greater efforts to provide legal pathways for migration, reducing the vulnerability of men who are forced to turn to traffickers to find work abroad. Finally, international cooperation is essential in dismantling the trafficking networks that profit from the exploitation of men, ensuring that labour markets are not complicit in modern slavery.

Until these changes are made, men trafficked for forced labour will continue to suffer in silence, hidden in plain sight, while the world benefits from the fruits of their exploitation.

Refugees and Economic Migrants: The Most Vulnerable Prey

Refugees and economic migrants, driven by war, persecution, and poverty, find themselves at the very heart of the human trafficking crisis. These individuals, already fleeing unimaginable hardship in their home countries, are often left with few alternatives when seeking safety and stability. Their vulnerability, combined with a deep sense of desperation, makes them prime targets for traffickers who see their plight as an opportunity for exploitation. For many of these migrants, their search for a better life becomes a cruel trap, leading them into a web of abuse, forced labour, or sexual exploitation.

The Refugee Crisis and Its Impact on Human Trafficking

The global refugee crisis, as discussed in Chapter 1, has significantly exacerbated human trafficking. With conflicts raging across the Middle East, North Africa, and parts of Asia, millions of people have been displaced, creating a vast population of refugees and internally displaced persons (IDPs). Many of these individuals are fleeing war-torn regions, where violence, persecution, and economic collapse have destroyed their lives and prospects. The civil wars in Syria, Afghanistan, and South Sudan, along with ongoing instability in Venezuela and parts of Sub-Saharan Africa, have contributed to a dramatic increase in the number of people seeking asylum in Europe, the United States, and other Western nations.

However, the sheer volume of displaced people has overwhelmed the international community's ability to provide adequate protection and assistance. Refugee camps, designed to offer temporary shelter, are often overcrowded, underfunded, and lacking in basic services such as food, water, and medical care. In these dire conditions, traffickers find fertile ground for recruitment, promising refugees to transport to safer countries or jobs abroad. Many refugees, facing limited options and desperate for a way out, willingly place their trust in these traffickers, unaware of the dangers that lie ahead.

Economic Migrants: Seeking Opportunity, Finding Exploitation

Economic migrants, while not fleeing direct persecution, are often equally vulnerable to trafficking. In regions plagued by chronic poverty, weak governance, and corruption, opportunities for legitimate work are scarce, and many are forced to seek employment abroad. The promise of better-paying jobs in wealthier nations is a powerful draw, and traffickers exploit this desire by offering transportation and forged documents, often at a steep price. These migrants, hailing from countries across Africa, Latin America, and Southeast Asia, embark on dangerous journeys, believing they are on the path to financial stability.

For example, economic migrants from countries like Nigeria, Senegal, and Eritrea often undertake perilous journeys across the Sahara Desert and the Mediterranean Sea, hoping to reach Europe. Similarly, Central American migrants from Honduras, El Salvador, and Guatemala embark on long treks through Mexico to the southern border of the United States, seeking work and safety. The routes themselves, as discussed in Chapter 2, are fraught with danger. Migrants face not only the physical risks of treacherous terrain, harsh weather, and overcrowded vehicles but also the ever-present threat of traffickers who promise safe passage in exchange for exorbitant fees.

The Exploitation of Vulnerability: Traffickers' Tactics

The desperation of both refugees and economic migrants creates a vulnerability that traffickers are quick to exploit. Whether on land or sea, traffickers operate with ruthless efficiency, providing smuggling services that often turn deadly. At the USA's southern border, for instance, migrants frequently pay thousands of dollars to traffickers, known as "coyotes," who promise to take them across the border safely. Many of these migrants are then crammed into the back of trucks, hidden in cargo containers, or forced to walk for days through the harsh desert, only to be abandoned or handed over to other criminal networks upon reaching the United States.

Similarly, the Mediterranean crossings, particularly between North Africa and Southern Europe, have become notorious for their high death tolls. Smugglers often pack hundreds of migrants onto unsafe, overcrowded boats, which are then abandoned at sea, leaving their passengers to either drown or be rescued by European authorities. Even for those who survive the crossing, the ordeal is far from over. Upon reaching European shores, many refugees and migrants are intercepted by traffickers who exploit their undocumented status and lack of resources, forcing them into labour or prostitution.

Traffickers often use deception as a primary tactic, promising jobs, safety, or a better life in exchange for compliance. Refugees and migrants are led to believe they will be offered legitimate work in the West whether in agriculture, domestic service, or construction. These promises are frequently supported by forged documents and elaborate recruitment schemes that appear credible, further enticing desperate individuals to accept the offer. But once these migrants arrive at their destination, the reality is starkly different. Traffickers confiscate their documents, leaving them without the means to prove their identity or legality, thus ensuring their total dependency on the trafficking network.

Refugees: Caught Between Conflict and Exploitation

Refugees are particularly vulnerable to trafficking due to their lack of legal status and the chaos of displacement. Separated from their families, homes, and support networks, many refugees are left in limbo stranded in foreign countries with no clear path to safety or stability. For refugee children, the risk is especially high. As discussed in Chapter 3, children who are separated from their parents during migration are at extreme risk of being trafficked for sexual exploitation or forced labour. These children, often without documents, become invisible to authorities, making them easy targets for traffickers operating within or near refugee camps.

In the case of Syrian refugees, for example, women and children fleeing the war have been particularly targeted by traffickers in neighbouring countries such as Lebanon, Turkey, and Jordan. In many cases, refugee women are lured into sex trafficking under the guise of employment, while children are forced into begging or menial labour. Similarly, Rohingya refugees from Myanmar, seeking safety in Bangladesh, have faced high levels of trafficking within refugee camps. The overcrowded conditions and lack of security in these camps make it difficult to prevent traffickers from preying on the most vulnerable.

Economic Migrants: Forced Labour and the Illusion of Work

For economic migrants, the promise of employment often becomes the nightmare of forced labour. Many of these migrants find themselves trapped in industries where their rights are systematically violated. In the agricultural fields of Southern Europe, for instance, African migrants are forced to work long hours for little pay, often under the threat of violence or deportation. In the United States, migrants from Central America face similar conditions, with many trafficked into construction, hospitality, or low-wage service jobs. Deprived of their legal status and fearing deportation, these migrants are unable to challenge their exploiters or seek protection from authorities.

Moreover, traffickers and unscrupulous employers exploit the complex nature of supply chains to mask the use of trafficked labour. This is particularly true in industries such as agriculture, construction, and manufacturing, where the demand for cheap labour creates opportunities for traffickers to operate with impunity. As discussed in Chapter 2, these industries benefit from the hidden exploitation of vulnerable migrants, who are forced to work under appalling conditions without the protection of labour laws or unions.

The Precarious Legal Status of Refugees and Migrants

A critical factor that facilitates the trafficking of refugees and economic migrants is their precarious legal status. Without proper documentation, they have little to no access to legal protections, making it easy for traffickers to manipulate and control them. In the West, many countries have implemented strict immigration policies that criminalise undocumented migrants, further driving them into the shadows. Refugees, who often arrive in host countries without the proper paperwork, are frequently denied asylum or forced to wait for years while their claims are processed. During this time, they are particularly vulnerable to traffickers, who exploit their legal limbo to force them into exploitative work or prostitution.

In the United States, for example, the backlog of asylum claims at the southern border has created a bottleneck, trapping thousands of refugees in legal limbo. This has led to an increase in the trafficking of these migrants, who are unable to work legally and are therefore more likely to fall into the hands of traffickers. Similarly, in Europe, the tightening of asylum policies has left many refugees stranded in camps or detention centres, where traffickers are known to recruit victims.

The Cycle of Exploitation: False Promises, Real Danger

The promises traffickers make to refugees and economic migrants of safety, employment, or a better life are almost always a cruel illusion. Instead of the stability they seek, many of these individuals find themselves caught in a cycle of exploitation and abuse. For women and girls, this often means being trafficked into the sex trade, while for men and boys, it means forced labour in harsh and dangerous industries. For all of these victims, the journey to the West, filled with hope and expectation, turns into a nightmare of exploitation from which escape is nearly impossible.

As outlined in Chapter 1, international efforts to combat human trafficking are often hampered by the sheer scale of the refugee and migration crises. International agencies, while working to protect these vulnerable populations, are overwhelmed by the number of displaced individuals and lack the resources to adequately address the issue. Meanwhile, traffickers continue to operate with impunity, taking advantage of weak governance, porous borders, and corrupt officials to exploit refugees and migrants with little fear of prosecution.

A Call for Stronger Protections

The trafficking of refugees and economic migrants is one of the most pressing human rights issues of our time, and addressing it requires a multi-faceted approach. First and foremost, international protections for refugees must be strengthened, with greater attention paid to those in legal limbo, particularly children. Governments must work together to provide safe and legal pathways for migrants and asylum seekers, reducing the need for them to turn to traffickers for help.

Moreover, the root causes of forced migration war, poverty, and persecution must be addressed through international cooperation and development efforts. Until these underlying issues are resolved, refugees and economic migrants will continue to be among the most vulnerable prey for traffickers, caught in a cycle of exploitation and abuse with no clear way out.

The Human Stories Behind the Statistics

It is easy to reduce human trafficking to numbers and statistics, but behind each data point is a story of unimaginable suffering. Victims come from every corner of the globe women fleeing conflict in Syria, children from rural villages in India, men seeking work from sub-Saharan Africa. Yet they all share a common thread: vulnerability. It is this vulnerability that traffickers exploit, turning hopes for a better life into nightmares of bondage and despair.

In this chapter, I hope to paint a vivid picture of who these victims are and how they end up in the clutches of traffickers. Their profiles are not simply demographic categories; they represent real lives interrupted by violence, deceit, and greed. The West, often seen as a beacon of opportunity, has become a final destination for many who are trapped in this modern form of slavery, unable to break free from the chains of their traffickers.

As we move forward in this book, we must remember that behind every route, every smuggling operation, and every statistic, a human is a person whose story has been hijacked by one of the darkest trades in modern history. Understanding their profiles is the first step in addressing the systemic factors that allow trafficking to thrive, as well as in devising effective strategies for rescue and rehabilitation.

I have sought to outline the distinct yet interconnected profiles of trafficked women from various regions. These stories, while deeply tragic, offer crucial insights into the global mechanisms of trafficking and the urgent need for targeted interventions. Understanding who these victims are is the first step in dismantling the systems that allow traffickers to thrive, as we move toward solutions that can protect the world's most vulnerable women from falling prey to this heinous trade. The challenges are immense, but so too is the urgency to act.

Chapter 4: The Machinery of Trafficking: Organised Crime Networks

Human trafficking is not an isolated crime; it is a deeply embedded, multifaceted enterprise driven by organised crime networks. These networks are the machinery of trafficking, coordinating the flow of vulnerable individuals across borders, continents, and jurisdictions, much like a well-oiled corporate entity. It is within these shadowy structures that traffickers find protection, resources, and a constant supply of desperate individuals, willing or unwitting, who are caught in their web. In this chapter, I aim to map out the key players within these networks, from large international syndicates to smaller, regional gangs, and demonstrate how their operations span the globe, feeding off the instability of weak governance, corruption, and the ever-present lure of financial gain.

The Organised Nature of Human Trafficking

Organised crime syndicates function much like multinational corporations, employing a highly structured, strategic approach that mirrors legitimate business models. Just as a global company seeks to maximise profits by streamlining supply chains, using intermediaries, and optimising distribution networks, so too do these criminal organisations. The product, however, is human lives, commodified and stripped of dignity, reduced to merchandise in a black-market economy that thrives on exploitation. Human trafficking is, therefore, an industry a coordinated and multifaceted operation where each cog in the machine has a distinct, deliberate role, from the initial recruitment of victims to their eventual exploitation in foreign lands.

Much like in a legitimate corporate structure, trafficking organisations are layered and compartmentalised. At the top sits a small cadre of leaders kingpins and crime bosses who orchestrate the overall strategy, set profit targets, and ensure the smooth running of their illicit ventures. These leaders seldom interact directly with the victims; they oversee operations remotely, leveraging the vast resources and networks at their disposal to move people across borders and continents. Like any CEO who relies on middle management to implement corporate directives, these syndicate leaders depend on intermediaries recruiters, transporters, and enforcers who operate at various levels within the organisation, ensuring that each stage of the trafficking process functions efficiently.

Recruiters act as the 'talent scouts' of the operation, targeting vulnerable populations, often in regions where economic desperation and political instability have made individuals easy prey. As I have previously discussed in Chapter 3, these victims come from war-torn areas, impoverished communities, or places affected by natural disasters. The recruiters, much like agents in legitimate industries, offer false promises of jobs, education, or even marriage in an attempt to lure their targets into the system. Their methods are highly adaptable, often using local knowledge to exploit cultural or societal norms. For example, in some regions, traffickers prey on young women under the guise of marriage proposals, while in others, they promise employment opportunities abroad to economically desperate men.

Once victims have been secured, the process moves into the 'logistics' phase, where transporters, analogous to shipping and supply chain managers, step in. These individuals or groups are responsible for moving the trafficked individuals across national and international borders. Like any efficient logistics operation, traffickers are skilled at identifying and exploiting weak points in the system. They take advantage of border vulnerabilities, using falsified documents, bribing officials, or relying on complex networks of human smugglers who specialise in moving people undetected. Transporters coordinate these movements, ensuring that victims are transferred from one safe house or transit point to the next, often through multiple countries and across treacherous routes.

Transport networks are not static but highly fluid, adapting to changes in law enforcement or border policies. Just as a company might adjust its supply routes in response to geopolitical developments, traffickers constantly shift their strategies to evade detection. For instance, as law enforcement tightens controls on one route, they may divert to less monitored pathways. As I mentioned in Chapter 2, routes from Latin America to the USA's southern border or across the Mediterranean into Europe are key examples of how traffickers constantly adapt, using land, sea, and air to transport their human cargo.

Enforcers play a critical role once victims arrive at their destination. They are akin to middle managers or security personnel in a corporation, responsible for ensuring that the 'product' in this case, the victims remains compliant and generates profit. This role involves the use of intimidation, violence, and coercion to maintain control over the trafficked individuals. Victims are often stripped of their identification, isolated from outside contact, and subjected to threats against their families, making escape nearly impossible. These enforcers oversee the day-to-day operations of exploitation, ensuring that victims are placed into labour camps, brothels, or forced labour situations that maximise the profits of the organisation.

Despite their similarities to legitimate corporations, what truly defines these crime syndicates is their adaptability. These organisations are not monolithic; they come in various shapes and sizes, from sprawling international networks to smaller, more localised groups. Large, transnational organisations, like those operating the human smuggling rings of Latin America or the mafia-driven trafficking operations in Eastern Europe, have vast resources at their disposal. They are highly coordinated, with operations spanning multiple countries, and they utilise sophisticated methods of communication and financial laundering to evade detection.

For instance, Latin American cartels that control human smuggling into the United States have diversified their portfolios, often engaging in drug and arms trafficking alongside human trafficking. They operate across borders, coordinating with local gangs and corrupt officials to ensure that their operations remain uninterrupted. Similarly, in Eastern Europe, mafia organisations run complex trafficking rings that move women and children into Western Europe for sexual exploitation. These operations are vast, involving multiple actors across different layers of the criminal underworld, and they are adept at leveraging corruption to keep law enforcement at bay.

On the other hand, smaller, regional outfits tend to operate within the confines of a particular locality or country. They may be less formal in structure but are no less effective in their ability to exploit local vulnerabilities. Often, these groups emerge in regions affected by conflict, poverty, or political instability, where governance is weak, and law enforcement is either too under-resourced or too corrupt to intervene. In such areas, trafficking outfits can operate with relative impunity, preying on the desperate and the displaced, often in collusion with local officials who turn a blind eye for financial gain.

What unites these varied groups is their structured, hierarchical nature. Whether it is a vast cartel operating across continents or a smaller gang exploiting a local conflict, these networks share a common feature: their ability to operate with precision and efficiency. Each actor within the network has a clear role, and the entire system is designed to maximise profits while minimising risk. In this sense, organised crime syndicates involved in human trafficking are not unlike global corporations, continuously adapting to new challenges and opportunities, all while generating immense financial gain from human misery.

This hierarchical structure also allows these networks to be highly adaptable. When law enforcement or international pressure makes one route or method too risky, these organisations quickly pivot, identifying new routes, partners, or victims. Like a business diversifying its supply chains in response to market fluctuations, traffickers can shift their operations to regions where governance is weaker or where law enforcement is less vigilant. This adaptability ensures their survival, even in the face of increased international scrutiny and efforts to combat trafficking.

In summary, organised crime networks engaged in human trafficking are highly sophisticated entities that mirror the operational frameworks of legitimate business models. From recruitment to exploitation, each phase of the trafficking process is meticulously planned and executed, with each actor playing a critical role. Whether these networks are vast, transnational syndicates or smaller, regional gangs, their ability to operate with precision, adaptability, and ruthlessness ensures that human trafficking remains one of the most profitable illicit industries in the world. By understanding these structures, we gain critical insight into how to disrupt their operations and, ultimately, dismantle the machinery that drives human exploitation.

The Players: Recruiters, Transporters, and Enforcers

Each trafficking network functions like a finely tuned machine, operating with a distinct division of labour, where every player within the organisation performs a vital role in ensuring the continuous flow of human capital. From recruitment to exploitation, this system runs efficiently, with the traffickers exploiting vulnerabilities at every stage. Each role in the trafficking chain is essential for the network's success, and understanding these roles provides a clearer picture of how these criminal organisations manage to operate across multiple regions and borders.

At the forefront of these operations are the recruiters, who serve as the "talent scouts" of the network. These individuals are often locals with intimate knowledge of the areas they target, enabling them to identify vulnerable individuals with ease. Posing as job agents, marriage brokers, or even humanitarian workers, recruiters approach potential victims with promises of employment, education, or a better life abroad. They capitalise on the desperation of their targets individuals who are often refugees, economic migrants, or those from impoverished backgrounds, as I discussed in **Chapter 3: Profiles of the Victims: Who Are They?** These victims are typically people who are searching for a way out of dire circumstances, and the recruiters offer them exactly what they believe to be their only chance for a better future.

However, the promises made by recruiters are nothing more than cruel deceptions. Job offers in foreign countries, educational scholarships, or arranged marriages are all fabrications designed to lure victims into a dangerous trap. Some recruiters even go so far as to create fake employment agencies or charitable organisations, building an air of legitimacy around their operations. These recruiters work closely with the rest of the trafficking network, ensuring a steady stream of human capital to be sold and exploited.

Once victims have been deceived and entrapped, they are handed over to the transporters, or smugglers, whose task is to move them across national borders. Transporters are the logistical experts of the operation, well-versed in navigating border controls and exploiting weak points in national security systems. Their methods range from relatively sophisticated operations, involving falsified documents and bribed officials, to far more brutal means, such as concealing victims in trucks, shipping containers, or overcrowded boats. The role of the transporter is crucial to the trafficking network, as the journey from source countries to destination countries often involves passing through multiple borders, each with its challenges.

As I outlined in **Chapter 2: The Routes to Exploitation: How Victims are Trafficked into the West**, these transporters are adept at using land, sea, and air routes to smuggle victims into Western countries. For example, victims from Africa and the Middle East are frequently transported across the Mediterranean, crammed into unseaworthy vessels, risking their lives on perilous waters. From Latin America, victims are smuggled across the USA's southern border, often forced to make treacherous journeys through deserts and rivers. In Eastern Europe, trafficking rings utilise hidden compartments in trucks or falsified passports to bring victims into the Schengen Area. Transporters are often part of larger smuggling rings, working in concert with corrupt border officials who are willing to turn a blind eye in exchange for financial incentives. This collaboration ensures the smooth transit of victims across borders and keeps the trafficking network operating without disruption.

Transporters, though not directly involved in the exploitation of victims, are critical to ensuring that the trafficking pipeline continues to function. Their deep knowledge of border regions, combined with their ability to adapt to changing enforcement measures, makes them indispensable to the syndicate. They remain flexible, often altering their routes and methods depending on law enforcement pressures, ensuring that the trafficking operations can continue to move people despite increased scrutiny.

The final stage in the trafficking process is controlled by the enforcers, or handlers, whose role is to manage and control the victims once they have arrived at their destination. These enforcers act as the muscle of the operation, using a combination of violence, coercion, and psychological manipulation to break down the victim's spirit and ensure compliance. Upon arrival, victims are often stripped of their identification documents and isolated from any form of external support, leaving them completely dependent on their captors. These individuals have nowhere to turn; they are trapped in a foreign country, often unable to speak the language, with no legal status and no means to escape.

The enforcers' primary objective is to ensure that the victims remain compliant and continue generating income for the trafficking network. This is achieved through a mix of intimidation and violence, with threats often directed not only at the victims themselves but also at their families back home. Victims are frequently subjected to physical abuse and psychological torment, which is designed to break their will and prevent them from resisting or attempting to flee. Enforcers also play a logistical role in the exploitation of victims, managing brothels, labour camps, or sweatshops where the victims are forced to work under inhumane conditions.

In cases of sexual exploitation, the enforcers control the daily operations of the brothels, ensuring that the victims are available to meet a constant stream of clients. They monitor the victims closely, using violence or the threat of violence to keep them in line. Victims in forced labour situations, on the other hand, are often placed in sweatshops or agricultural fields where they work long hours for little or no pay. In these settings, the enforcers oversee the victims' movements, making sure they remain productive and compliant. The victims are not only denied their freedom but also their basic human dignity, treated as nothing more than disposable commodities in a system designed to extract maximum profit.

What makes the enforcers particularly effective is their ability to instil fear and control through a mix of brute force and psychological manipulation. Victims are often told that they will be handed over to the authorities if they attempt to escape, a threat that carries significant weight for those without legal status or proper documentation. This fear of deportation or imprisonment, combined with the trauma of violence, keeps the victims trapped in the cycle of exploitation.

The division of labour within these trafficking networks ensures that each stage of the process operates with ruthless efficiency. From the recruiters who prey on the vulnerable to the transporters who move them across borders and the enforcers who maintain control, every player performs a critical role in the success of the operation. Each stage is designed to isolate and disempower the victims, making escape or resistance nearly impossible.

This well-coordinated operation is what allows human trafficking to persist on such a massive scale. As with any business model, each actor in the network is motivated by profit, and the traffickers go to great lengths to ensure that their "product" human lives continue to flow through the system. By understanding this division of labour, we can better comprehend how these networks function and how to target the different actors within the system. Each role in this process recruitment, transport, and enforcement must be dismantled if we are to effectively combat human trafficking and bring an end to this modern form of slavery.

Corruption: The Lubricant of Trafficking Operations

Corruption is the lifeblood of organised crime networks, and it is one of the most critical elements that allow human trafficking to thrive on such a vast and enduring scale. While traffickers prey on the vulnerable and manipulate systems to achieve their ends, it is corruption rooted in both source and destination countries that provides them with the impunity to operate. In regions where governance is weak, law enforcement is underfunded, and political instability reigns, traffickers find fertile ground to recruit, transport, and exploit their victims. This chapter explores the mechanisms by which corruption fuels trafficking operations, from the collusion of local officials in impoverished regions to the complicity of border guards and customs officers in the developed world.

Weak governance in source countries is the first link in the chain that traffickers exploit. Many of these countries are burdened by a mix of poverty, political instability, and weak law enforcement conditions that create ideal opportunities for criminal networks to flourish. In regions where economic despair is rampant, traffickers find a steady supply of vulnerable individuals desperate for a way out. Governments in these areas, often battling corruption within their ranks, struggle to combat organised crime due to the lack of resources or political will. Police forces, underpaid and understaffed, are often powerless to resist the financial allure that traffickers offer. In some cases, officials are not just passive bystanders but active participants in trafficking operations, taking bribes in exchange for turning a blind eye or facilitating the process.

For instance, in many parts of Africa, Asia, and Eastern Europe, it is common for border officials to accept bribes to allow traffickers to smuggle individuals across borders without facing scrutiny. Similarly, local police may be paid off to ignore suspicious activities, such as the movement of large groups of people or the operation of illegal brothels and labour camps. These officials often justify their involvement by pointing to the systemic poverty they face, but their complicity fuels an industry that profits from human misery. This culture of impunity allows trafficking operations to continue unabated, as the traffickers know they can rely on the cooperation or, at the very least, the inaction of local authorities.

However, the corruption that enables human trafficking is not confined to source countries. In many destination countries, particularly in the West, traffickers find accomplices among officials who are willing to take bribes in exchange for allowing trafficked individuals to enter the country illegally. These destination countries, while generally having stronger law enforcement and governance structures, are not immune to corruption. Border guards, immigration officers, and customs officials can be bought, allowing traffickers to circumvent the very systems designed to prevent such crimes.

The porous southern border of the United States and the Mediterranean crossings into Europe, as mentioned in **Chapter 2: The Routes to Exploitation: How Victims are Trafficked into the West**, are prime examples of how traffickers exploit weak oversight to their advantage. At the USA's southern border, for instance, traffickers frequently bribe border agents to smuggle migrants and trafficking victims into the country. In some cases, entire smuggling networks have been uncovered where officials were deeply embedded within the criminal operations, turning a blind eye to illegal border crossings or even facilitating the process themselves. The sheer volume of migrants attempting to cross into the United States makes it difficult for authorities to police every entry point effectively, and this strain creates opportunities for corruption to take root.

Similarly, in Europe, the Mediterranean Sea has become a major route for traffickers smuggling victims from Africa and the Middle East. With hundreds of thousands of migrants attempting to reach European shores each year, traffickers often exploit the chaos by bribing officials or using falsified documents to pass victims off as legitimate refugees. The asylum systems in many European countries, overwhelmed by the sheer number of applicants, are vulnerable to abuse. Traffickers exploit bureaucratic loopholes, submitting false asylum claims or manipulating the system to move victims into the country under the guise of legal migration. Once inside the borders of destination countries, these victims often disappear into the underground economy, forced into labour or sexual exploitation while remaining largely invisible to the public and law enforcement.

In both source and destination countries, traffickers rely on corrupt officials to facilitate their operations. Whether it is a local police officer accepting a bribe to ignore a trafficking ring or a border guard allowing illegal crossings, these officials create an environment where traffickers can operate with impunity. The financial incentives for corruption are significant. Human trafficking generates billions of dollars in profits each year, and traffickers are willing to spend significant sums to ensure the success of their operations. For officials working in underfunded or poorly regulated environments, the temptation to accept bribes can be overwhelming, especially when the alternative may be low wages and little hope of advancement.

Corruption is not just about individuals taking bribes, however. In many cases, it is systemic, with entire networks of officials working together to protect and enable traffickers. In some countries, law enforcement, immigration, and political officials may all be complicit, forming a web of corruption that is nearly impossible to untangle. This systemic corruption creates a culture of impunity, where traffickers know they can operate without fear of prosecution or interference. The victims of trafficking are often the ones who suffer the most in these environments, as they have nowhere to turn for help. Even if they manage to escape their traffickers, the authorities may not be willing or able to assist them due to the pervasive corruption within the system.

The role of corruption in human trafficking extends beyond the borders of source and destination countries. In many transit countries nations that serve as stopping points for traffickers moving victims across continents, corruption is also rampant. These countries, often with weak governance structures and porous borders, serve as key waypoints for traffickers as they move their victims from one region to another. Transit countries in North Africa, the Balkans, and Southeast Asia, for example, are notorious for the corruption that allows trafficking networks to operate with little resistance. In these regions, traffickers bribe officials to allow them to pass through checkpoints, use falsified documents, or gain access to transportation networks. Without the complicity of corrupt officials in these transit countries, it would be far more difficult for traffickers to move victims across such vast distances.

Corruption also facilitates the financial side of human trafficking. Traffickers must launder the billions of dollars they make from their operations, and corrupt financial institutions or officials are often instrumental in helping them do so. Banks, money transfer services, and even cryptocurrency exchanges can be exploited to move illicit funds across borders, making it difficult for law enforcement to track the profits of trafficking rings. In some cases, traffickers may bribe financial regulators or bank employees to ignore suspicious transactions, allowing them to continue laundering their profits without detection.

In conclusion, corruption is a fundamental enabler of human trafficking. From the impoverished villages where victims are recruited, to the border crossings where they are smuggled, to the sweatshops and brothels where they are exploited, corruption permeates every stage of the trafficking process. Weak governance, systemic poverty, and underfunded law enforcement create the conditions in which trafficking thrives, but it is the collusion of corrupt officials that allows these operations to flourish without fear of retribution. Combating human trafficking will require not only targeting the traffickers themselves but also addressing the culture of corruption that shields them from justice. Only by dismantling the networks of complicit officials and strengthening governance can we hope to bring an end to this modern form of slavery.

Financial Incentives: The Lucrative Business of Human Trafficking

At its core, human trafficking is an enterprise motivated by one thing: profit. The financial incentives that drive this illicit trade are staggering, with the global market for human beings generating an estimated $150 billion annually. This figure places trafficking alongside drug smuggling and arms dealing as one of the most lucrative illegal industries in the world. Traffickers view human lives as commodity assets to be bought, sold, and exploited for the highest possible return. It is a system of exploitation in its most brutal form, where the victims are reduced to mere financial calculations in a criminal business model that is designed for maximum profitability and minimal risk.

The economics of human trafficking are grounded in the same principles that drive any other industry: supply and demand. Traffickers prey on individuals who have limited economic opportunities, exploiting their desperation for a better life. As I discussed in **Chapter 3: Profiles of the Victims**, those most vulnerable to trafficking are refugees, economic migrants, and people from impoverished or unstable regions. These individuals are often lured by promises of employment, safety, or a brighter future, only to find themselves trapped in a cycle of abuse and exploitation. Once ensnared, escape is almost impossible, as the traffickers exert control through violence, debt bondage, and the removal of identity documents.

The demand side of the equation is driven by the insatiable appetite for cheap labour, sexual services, and other forms of exploitation in both developed and developing nations. Industries ranging from agriculture and construction to domestic service and prostitution depend on trafficked individuals to meet their needs for inexpensive and compliant labour. This is especially true in sectors where legal protections for workers are weak or non-existent, making it easier for traffickers to operate undetected. The traffickers' profit by supplying this "human capital" to meet demand, and their profit margins are only enhanced by the fact that they often pay nothing to their victims, who are essentially forced to work for free under conditions of modern slavery.

Human trafficking does not operate in isolation. For many organised crime syndicates, it is merely one of several revenue streams in a larger portfolio of illegal activities. Traffickers may also be involved in drug smuggling, arms trafficking, money laundering, and a host of other criminal ventures. This diversification of operations not only increases their financial stability but also makes it more difficult for law enforcement agencies to dismantle their networks. When law enforcement targets one aspect of the operation, such as drug trafficking, the criminal organisation can continue generating income through other activities, including human trafficking. This ability to shift focus between illegal enterprises helps traffickers remain resilient and adaptable in the face of police pressure.

Moreover, these criminal organisations have become increasingly sophisticated over time. They have adopted the operational efficiency of multinational corporations, using advanced technology to evade detection and coordinate activities across borders. For example, traffickers now use encrypted communications, dark web marketplaces, and cryptocurrencies to facilitate their operations and move money through untraceable channels. These technological advancements have made it more difficult for law enforcement to track the financial flows associated with human trafficking, which are often hidden among legitimate transactions or laundered through complex international networks. The use of online recruitment tactics has also grown, with traffickers targeting victims through social media platforms, job listing sites, and other digital spaces, further complicating efforts to identify and intercept trafficking operations.

As trafficking rings expand their operations across continents, their ability to coordinate activities on a global scale becomes another advantage. They often exploit the gaps in international cooperation, taking advantage of differing legal frameworks, enforcement priorities, and levels of government commitment to combat trafficking. This fractured global approach, as I explored in **Chapter 1: Unveiling the Crisis: A Global Overview of Human Trafficking**, plays directly into the hands of traffickers. International conventions such as the Palermo Protocol, while crucial in setting standards and guidelines for combating trafficking, rely on national governments to enforce these laws. However, enforcement efforts are often underfunded, under-resourced, and fragmented, allowing traffickers to slip through the cracks.

One of the key challenges facing enforcement agencies is the sheer scale and complexity of organised crime networks involved in trafficking. Many of these organisations are deeply entrenched in local economies and political systems, making it difficult for law enforcement to gain the intelligence needed to disrupt their activities. As discussed earlier in **Chapter 4**, corruption plays a significant role in protecting these networks, with corrupt officials providing traffickers with the cover they need to operate freely. In some cases, traffickers are so embedded in local communities that they can manipulate or even co-opt law enforcement, further undermining efforts to bring them to justice.

In addition to corruption, traffickers benefit from the differing legal frameworks across countries. In some nations, penalties for human trafficking are relatively lenient, making it a low-risk, high-reward endeavour for criminals. In others, the legal system may lack the resources or expertise to prosecute trafficking cases effectively. Even in countries with strong anti-trafficking laws, the focus is often on prosecuting low-level operatives such as recruiters or transporters while the masterminds behind the networks remain untouchable. This inability to target the upper echelons of trafficking organisations limits the effectiveness of law enforcement efforts, as dismantling the lower tiers of a trafficking network does little to disrupt the overall operation.

Furthermore, trafficking networks are highly adaptable, constantly evolving to exploit new opportunities and circumvent law enforcement efforts. When one route becomes too risky or well-monitored, traffickers simply shift to another. For instance, as discussed in **Chapter 2: The Routes to Exploitation: How Victims are Trafficked into the West**, the well-known Mediterranean crossings into Europe have seen periodic declines in traffic due to increased surveillance and patrols. However, traffickers have adapted by shifting their focus to land routes through the Balkans or finding new sea routes to avoid detection. Similarly, in the United States, traffickers have adjusted their tactics at the southern border, using tunnels, drones, and other means to bypass enhanced border security.

The financial incentives driving human trafficking are compounded by the relative impunity traffickers enjoy. With enforcement efforts hampered by limited resources, corruption, and the sheer complexity of the problem, traffickers operate with little fear of significant consequences. Even when arrests are made, prosecution and conviction rates remain low in many countries, and traffickers often find ways to continue their operations from behind bars or quickly re-establish their networks after serving minimal prison sentences. The financial rewards of human trafficking far outweigh the risks for those involved, perpetuating a cycle of exploitation that seems nearly impossible to break.

In conclusion, the financial motivations behind human trafficking cannot be overstated. Organised crime syndicates, driven by the immense profits available from trafficking, operate with the same efficiency and sophistication as legitimate businesses. The diversification of their operations, combined with the use of advanced technology and the ability to exploit global legal and enforcement gaps, makes it increasingly difficult to combat human trafficking effectively. While international conventions like the Palermo Protocol set out important frameworks for combating this global crisis, the fractured nature of the global response allows traffickers to continue profiting from the exploitation of human lives. To truly tackle the problem, governments must prioritise cooperation, funding, and enforcement efforts that are commensurate with the scale of the trafficking industry. Only then can we hope to dismantle the financial incentives that make human trafficking such a thriving global trade.

Exploiting Conflict Zones and Lawless Regions

The nexus between organised crime and political instability is one of the most critical factors that sustain human trafficking on a global scale. Traffickers thrive in regions where governance is weak, and law enforcement lacks the resources, authority, or even the willingness to intervene. In environments where state institutions have collapsed, or are under severe strain due to conflict, corruption, or economic despair, trafficking networks operate freely, often with impunity. This lawlessness, combined with the vulnerability of populations caught in these unstable conditions, creates the perfect breeding ground for traffickers to flourish.

Regions suffering from protracted conflict, such as parts of Africa and the Middle East, are particularly fertile ground for trafficking networks. Wars, civil unrest, and insurgencies displace millions of people, creating a vast and vulnerable pool of potential victims.

Refugees fleeing violence, persecution, or economic hardship often find themselves with few options. As I discussed in **Chapter 3: Profiles of the Victims**, displaced persons, whether in refugee camps or attempting to cross borders, are some of the most at-risk populations. Traffickers prey on their desperation, offering them a deceptive way out of their plight, whether it be the promise of employment, safe passage to a more stable country, or even protection from further violence.

In these war-torn regions, traffickers often operate with the tacit approval or active cooperation of local militias, warlords, and even government forces. These actors may see human trafficking as a way to finance their operations, using forced labour or sexual exploitation as additional streams of income in their efforts to maintain power or fund their ongoing conflicts. For example, in parts of Sub-Saharan Africa, armed groups have been known to abduct women and children, forcing them into labour or sexual slavery. The rise of terrorist organisations such as Boko Haram in Nigeria or ISIS in the Middle East has shown how trafficking can be weaponised, with kidnapped victims sold into slavery or used as political leverage. In these contexts, trafficking becomes not just an economic crime but a tool of political control and violence.

Fragile states where the rule of law is tenuous provide another layer of opportunity for traffickers. In these countries, where governance structures are weak, and law enforcement is either underfunded or corrupt, trafficking networks can operate with virtual impunity. In countries such as Libya, which has been destabilised by years of civil war, traffickers exploit the chaos to control migrant routes through the country. With no effective central government to enforce law and order, criminal syndicates, smugglers, and traffickers have set up their parallel systems of governance, controlling entire territories and extracting profits from the suffering of migrants passing through.

In these fragile environments, traffickers are often deeply embedded in local power structures, making it even more difficult for external forces, such as international law enforcement or humanitarian organisations, to intervene. Corruption among local officials only exacerbates the problem. As I highlighted earlier in **Chapter 4**, corrupt border guards, police, and immigration officials frequently turn a blind eye to trafficking operations in exchange for bribes or personal gain. In some cases, they are directly involved in these operations, facilitating the transport of victims across borders or helping traffickers evade detection by law enforcement. This collusion between traffickers and local officials perpetuates a culture of impunity, where the traffickers can continue their operations without fear of being prosecuted.

One of the most tragic aspects of this nexus between organised crime and political instability is the false hope traffickers offer to their victims. In destabilised regions, where governments cannot provide basic services, let alone opportunities for economic advancement, traffickers present themselves as the only viable solution to those seeking to escape poverty or violence. They promise jobs, safety, or a new life in Europe or North America, preying on the desperation of people who have no other options. As I explored in **Chapter 3**, these victims are often deceived into believing they are embarking on a legitimate journey, only to find themselves ensnared in the machinery of trafficking. Women and girls may be promised jobs as domestic workers or in the service industry, only to be forced into prostitution upon arrival. Men may be lured by the prospect of construction or agricultural work, only to be trapped in exploitative conditions, unable to leave due to the confiscation of their documents or threats of violence.

The political instability in these regions is not limited to source countries alone; it extends to transit and destination countries as well. Trafficking networks exploit porous borders and weak law enforcement across entire regions, creating a vast transnational web of human smuggling. As I explored in **Chapter 2: The Routes to Exploitation**, routes through North Africa, the Balkans, and Central America are constantly shifting as traffickers adapt to new challenges or opportunities. For example, when the Mediterranean became more closely monitored by European authorities, traffickers shifted their operations to less well-guarded routes through the Balkans or across the Sahara Desert. Similarly, in the Americas, traffickers use increasingly sophisticated means to evade border security along the USA's southern border, moving people through remote areas or via tunnels and concealed vehicles.

In this way, trafficking networks are not only flexible but resilient, able to thrive in regions where state control is weakest. Political instability often works to their advantage. The collapse of law and order means there are fewer obstacles to their operations, and in some cases, they can even establish themselves as alternative sources of authority in regions abandoned by the state. In Libya, for example, traffickers control detention centres for migrants and operate open-air slave markets, all while local militias and warlords profit from the trade. This level of impunity is possible only in environments where governance has collapsed and the rule of law is essentially non-existent.

Even in more stable destination countries, political instability or fragmented systems of governance can create loopholes that traffickers exploit. As I mentioned in **Chapter 4**, the complicity of corrupt officials in Western countries whether through bribery or bureaucratic inefficiency allows traffickers to continue bringing victims into the country. Furthermore, traffickers exploit the complexities of asylum systems and immigration laws, using them as cover for their illicit operations. Migrants and refugees, who are often fleeing genuine persecution, are manipulated into becoming commodities in this illicit trade. Traffickers can infiltrate the legal channels designed to help those in need, further blurring the lines between legitimate migration and trafficking.

In conclusion, the link between organised crime and political instability plays a central role in the persistence of human trafficking. Traffickers exploit weak governance, corruption, and conflict to their advantage, establishing themselves in regions where state control has disintegrated. They prey on the vulnerable those displaced by war, poverty, or persecution and deceive them with false promises of safety and prosperity. This cycle of exploitation is sustained by the broader political and economic chaos in these regions, making it incredibly difficult to break. Until governments and international institutions can address the root causes of instability conflict, poverty, and corruption the machinery of trafficking will continue to grind on, feeding on the suffering of the most vulnerable members of society.

The machinery of human trafficking is vast and complex, driven by organised crime networks that span continents and operate with ruthless efficiency. These networks exploit the vulnerabilities of individuals, the weaknesses of governments, and the global demand for cheap labour and sexual exploitation. As we continue to explore the modern-day realities of human trafficking, it is crucial to understand the inner workings of these criminal enterprises. By dismantling the machinery that drives trafficking, we can begin to address the root causes and, ultimately, reduce the global scale of this atrocity.

In the following chapters, I will delve deeper into the socio-economic factors that contribute to the rise of human trafficking, as well as the international efforts to combat these crime networks. The path to ending human trafficking is fraught with challenges but understanding how organised crime networks function is the first step toward breaking the cycle.

Chapter 5: The Role of Corruption: How Governance and Law Enforcement Fail

Corruption is the silent enabler of human trafficking, acting as both a shield for traffickers and a wall of impunity that prevents justice from being served. As I continue the exploration of this global crisis, it is essential to understand the pivotal role that corruption plays at every level, both in source and destination countries. Without addressing the corruption that fuels this trade, any anti-trafficking efforts remain, at best, superficial.

In the previous chapters, I outlined the intricacies of human trafficking examining the machinery of organised crime (Chapter 4), the victims who are ensnared in its web (Chapter 3), and the routes used to smuggle these individuals into the West (Chapter 2). But the dark reality is that behind each successful trafficking operation, there are corrupt officials whose complicity allows the traffickers to continue their work unchallenged. These officials, whether bribed or actively complicit, are part of the same systemic breakdown that perpetuates this industry.

The Scale of Corruption in Human Trafficking

Corruption in human trafficking manifests itself in insidious and varied ways across the globe. The financial power of traffickers, coupled with the vulnerabilities within legal and political systems, creates a fertile environment for corruption to thrive. Local-level law enforcement and border officials are often bribed to ignore trafficking activities, providing traffickers with a direct path to carry on their operations unimpeded. These are not isolated incidents but a systemic issue where traffickers wield money as a weapon, manipulating the very institutions meant to safeguard against their crimes.

The Pull of Financial Incentives and Systemic Vulnerabilities in Source Countries

Corruption is particularly prevalent in source countries, where traffickers exploit weaknesses in governance, underfunded law enforcement, and the economic desperation of officials. Many of these countries struggle with political instability, often due to internal conflicts, weak economies, or transitioning governments that lack established frameworks to support anti-corruption measures. In this climate, the promise of financial gain becomes a significant motivating factor for officials to turn a blind eye. Local law enforcement, who may go months without receiving full salaries, can be tempted into accepting bribes simply as a means of survival. For these officials, cooperating with traffickers may offer financial security that their positions within the government cannot provide.

Some officials may also be active participants in trafficking networks, acting as facilitators rather than passive bystanders. In nations with fragile political systems, the influence of traffickers may extend to the highest echelons of government. Here, high-ranking officials may use their power to shield trafficking operations, either through direct complicity or by weakening legal frameworks that would otherwise hinder traffickers. These officials may obstruct investigations, prevent the passage of anti-trafficking legislation, or make concessions to traffickers in exchange for lucrative kickbacks. The close relationship between traffickers and officials in these areas, as I outlined in Chapter 4, allows traffickers to operate with impunity, exploiting the very systems that are supposed to contain them.

Complicity in Fragile States and the Exploitation of Political Weaknesses

In some cases, entire governments may become so entangled in trafficking networks that distinguishing between official and criminal activity becomes nearly impossible. When a state lacks the resources or political will to combat trafficking, traffickers are often seen as economic assets rather than criminals. This is especially true in conflict-ridden regions, where the line between legitimate governance and organised crime becomes blurred, and trafficking is tacitly accepted as a means of economic survival. Here, traffickers hold a unique form of influence; they control wealth, power, and resources in regions otherwise plagued by poverty and unemployment. Officials in these fragile states may view traffickers not as criminals, but as an economic boon, often justifying their actions as a necessary evil in the absence of a more stable economy.

Furthermore, in countries where corruption has permeated every level of governance, traffickers can dictate terms to local authorities with minimal fear of repercussion. Officials are often coerced or co-opted into supporting trafficking operations, either by direct financial incentives or through veiled threats. Those who attempt to resist are frequently subjected to intimidation, and in extreme cases, they or their families may be targeted by traffickers as a means of silencing dissent. Consequently, the entire structure of anti-trafficking efforts becomes compromised, leaving victims unprotected and vulnerable.

Corruption in Destination Countries: A Different Form of Compromise

Corruption is not restricted to source countries; destination countries are also plagued by it, albeit in different forms. While Western political and legal systems may be more robust, corruption still thrives in certain sectors, particularly along borders and within immigration systems. Traffickers rely on cooperation from border control agents and immigration officers to successfully smuggle victims into destination countries. Bribes offered to these officials serve as incentives to allow traffickers and their victims to cross borders without a thorough inspection.

For example, in high-profile cases along the United States-Mexico border, border agents have been implicated in smuggling operations, accepting bribes in exchange for allowing traffickers to pass through checkpoints without interference. Similarly, in the Mediterranean region, some officials in Southern European countries have reportedly accepted pay-offs to facilitate the smuggling of individuals from Africa and the Middle East. These are not isolated incidents but indicators of a broader, systemic failure that traffickers are quick to exploit. This aligns with the insights on trafficking routes I detailed in Chapter 2, where traffickers continuously adapt their pathways and methods to evade law enforcement.

Beyond border control, law enforcement and immigration officials in destination countries have also been implicated in trafficking networks, often through subtle forms of cooperation that go undetected. Some officers are known to accept payments in exchange for dismissing trafficking charges or for failing to investigate suspected cases. This corruption within law enforcement hampers victim rescue efforts, allowing traffickers to evade punishment and continue their operations without fear of intervention. In countries with strict immigration controls, traffickers may find it advantageous to form relationships with corrupt immigration officials, who can offer insider knowledge on enforcement schedules, investigation tactics, and legal loopholes, further enabling traffickers to remain one step ahead of the law.

High-Level Obstruction and the Dilution of Anti-Trafficking Laws

Corruption in destination countries often reaches beyond law enforcement, extending to the judicial system and high-ranking government officials who have the power to shape legal frameworks and policies. In some Western countries, traffickers have been known to influence officials at this level, using bribes to weaken or delay anti-trafficking legislation that could jeopardise their operations. This type of high-level obstruction can take many forms: some officials may actively lobby against the passage of strict trafficking laws, while others may dilute existing legislation to reduce the severity of penalties associated with trafficking crimes.

These actions create significant barriers to prosecuting traffickers and protecting victims. The judicial process becomes so convoluted that even when traffickers are apprehended, they face only minimal consequences. This serves to embolden trafficking networks, who view such legal leniency as an implicit endorsement of their activities. Victims, already traumatised by their experiences, are forced to confront a judicial system that may offer little protection and may even punish them for their undocumented status. This lack of recourse often leaves them hesitant to cooperate with authorities or to seek justice, fearing further harm or deportation.

Implications for International Anti-Trafficking Efforts

The presence of corruption across source, transit, and destination countries complicates international anti-trafficking efforts. International agreements, such as the Palermo Protocol, aim to promote cooperation among nations in combating trafficking. However, these protocols rely on each country's willingness and ability to implement their provisions effectively. When corruption is entrenched, these international agreements often fail in practice, as corrupt officials undermine enforcement mechanisms, sabotaging the work of dedicated anti-trafficking agencies.

For instance, border enforcement initiatives that should form the first line of defence against trafficking often become a weak link in the chain due to bribery. Likewise, international financial regulations intended to trace trafficking-related transactions are easily circumvented with the aid of corrupt banking officials, who are either complicit or apathetic. This financial complicity allows traffickers to launder profits with impunity, sustaining their operations and allowing their financial networks to grow. As I highlighted in Chapter 4, organised trafficking networks are often highly adaptive, using sophisticated financial manoeuvres to stay under the radar. Corrupt officials within financial institutions and government agencies make it possible for traffickers to exploit these regulatory blind spots.

Moving Forward: Tackling Corruption as the Root Cause

To truly address the issue of human trafficking, it is essential to tackle corruption at its roots. Anti-trafficking initiatives need to be accompanied by anti-corruption measures, focusing not only on increasing penalties for corrupt officials but also on creating transparent systems of accountability. This includes establishing independent bodies that oversee the actions of border control agents, law enforcement, and high-ranking officials. Equally important is international cooperation and intelligence-sharing, ensuring that corrupt practices do not go unnoticed, even across borders.

Addressing corruption will require sustained efforts and an unwavering commitment from governments, organisations, and the international community. This involves creating both preventive measures and punitive repercussions for those who facilitate trafficking through their complicity. Only by addressing the corrosive impact of corruption can we hope to dismantle the trafficking networks that continue to thrive unchecked. The battle against trafficking cannot be won solely on the front lines; it must also be waged within the political and legal systems that traffickers have co-opted to their advantage.

Border Officials: Gatekeepers or Gate-Openers?

In *Chapter 2: The Routes to Exploitation*, I outlined the extensive network of land, sea, and air routes traffickers use to smuggle victims into Western countries. This complex web of pathways cutting across Latin America, Africa, Eastern Europe, and beyond serves as a lifeline for traffickers, allowing them to transport victims from impoverished or war-torn regions to wealthier nations where demand drives this illicit trade. However, the very success of these trafficking operations rests not merely on logistical planning but heavily on the complicity of corrupt officials at critical junctures along these routes. Border officials, tasked with preventing unlawful crossings, become the gatekeepers who, through bribery and collusion, transform these borders from barriers into mere checkpoints in a global trafficking circuit.

Corruption Along African Trafficking Routes: Gatekeepers of Exploitation

In Africa, border officials play a pivotal role in enabling trafficking operations. Key routes in North, West, and East Africa are rife with corruption, where traffickers move people across national boundaries with a mix of forged or stolen documents, or in some cases, without any identification at all. This system is so pervasive that many border officials are not merely passive participants; they actively collaborate with traffickers, creating a transactional relationship in which human lives become currency. For instance, officials may accept bribes not only in cash but also in favours or promises of security traffickers offering protection or political sway in return for passage. In countries with weak central governance, such as those affected by protracted conflict or economic instability, border officials may view collaboration with traffickers as a steady, even essential, supplement to their meagre incomes, thereby embedding corruption deep within local governance structures.

In regions like the Sahel and along the central migration corridor stretching from sub-Saharan Africa towards North Africa, corruption is so endemic that traffickers operate with relative transparency, emboldened by the expectation of police cooperation. When a border official is paid off, entire checkpoints become, in essence, open doors, allowing traffickers to move large numbers of people without fear of interference. This collusion extends beyond local checkpoints; organised trafficking networks leverage their financial power to gain influence at higher levels of governance. Here, anti-trafficking regulations are diluted, investigations obstructed, and officials in crucial positions incentivised to turn a blind eye or even facilitate trafficking.

The Mediterranean Crossings: Complicity from the Source to the Shores of Europe

The Mediterranean crossing from North Africa into Europe represents one of the deadliest yet most active routes for human trafficking. Libya stands out as a key launching point for traffickers, where the collapse of central authority following years of political upheaval has created a lawless landscape. In this vacuum, trafficking networks have flourished, with certain border officials and local authorities actively involved in the trade. In regions such as these, bribery becomes less a matter of extra income and more an essential component of the local economy. Border officials in Libya, for example, receive regular payments from traffickers, with some even reportedly collecting a form of "passage fee" for each victim that passes through their jurisdiction.

Libya's fractured political landscape provides traffickers with multiple points of entry into Europe, each overseen by local officials seeking to profit. Here, traffickers use corruption as a tool, funnelling substantial payments to authorities who ensure that boats filled with desperate migrants and trafficked individuals are permitted to depart without question. These payments, often reaching officials with ties to militia groups or local governing bodies, create a system where government and trafficker interests are inseparably intertwined. For traffickers, the officials' complicity offers a layer of security; for the officials, it represents an indispensable income stream in an otherwise unstable political and economic environment. This reality turns the Mediterranean crossing into a recurring humanitarian crisis, where corruption ensures a constant flow of trafficked individuals despite substantial international efforts to curb trafficking.

Latin America and the United States Southern Border: Corruption and Collusion

While corruption is often more pervasive in countries with weaker governance systems, even well-resourced nations like the United States are not immune. The southern border with Mexico has become a critical focal point for human trafficking into the United States. Here, traffickers exploit not only the physical border but also human vulnerabilities, leveraging corruption to secure passage into American territory. While the United States has a robust border security framework, cases of corruption within its ranks demonstrate how traffickers' financial influence can infiltrate even the most fortified systems.

Numerous incidents have implicated American border agents in scandals where traffickers have paid them off to facilitate crossings. Some officials accept bribes to overlook border crossings or to provide traffickers with information on enforcement schedules, allowing traffickers to bypass patrols. Although such cases are not as frequent as in nations with weaker institutional controls, they highlight a fundamental reality of human trafficking: that corruption does not respect borders or governance levels. In Mexico, which serves as a transit country for trafficked individuals en route to the United States, corruption is even more rampant. Traffickers routinely bribe Mexican officials, ensuring that checkpoints along the journey are either unmanned or accessible with the proper financial "inducements."

The Erosion of Border Security and Legal Accountability

When border officials in multiple countries whether at sea crossings, land borders, or airports participate in corruption, the very concept of border security is compromised. Corruption essentially dismantles border security measures, rendering legal efforts and international agreements ineffective. This impacts the entire spectrum of anti-trafficking efforts, from surveillance and interdiction to victim rescue and criminal prosecution. Each corrupted checkpoint, port, or border crossing allows traffickers to exploit legal loopholes, effectively dismantling any semblance of a cohesive international response to human trafficking.

Additionally, corrupt practices among border officials erode public trust in government institutions, reducing the willingness of trafficked individuals and their advocates to cooperate with law enforcement. This mistrust hampers investigations, creating a cycle in which traffickers evade capture, authorities lose credibility, and victims remain trapped within a system that fails to protect them. As I examined in *Chapter 1*, a cohesive international approach to combating human trafficking hinges on accountability. When border officials accept bribes, the entire framework of laws and conventions that Western and international bodies rely upon to combat trafficking is undermined. Furthermore, the funds traffickers pay to corrupt officials often come directly from the exploitation of victims, meaning that every bribe not only facilitates trafficking but also financially incentivises future exploitation.

Towards a Solution: Addressing Corruption Along Trafficking Routes

The fight against human trafficking necessitates a parallel battle against corruption, particularly among border officials. This will require more than tokenistic measures; robust oversight and anti-corruption initiatives must be an intrinsic part of every anti-trafficking strategy. Some potential approaches include increasing transparency, conducting regular audits, and enhancing the surveillance of border control activities. International cooperation is also critical, as traffickers adapt to exploit weaknesses in even the most sophisticated border systems. Intelligence-sharing, joint task forces and training initiatives that involve both source and destination countries could form a significant part of a stronger, more cohesive strategy.

However, beyond monitoring and accountability, improving the socioeconomic conditions of border officials particularly in poorer nations is essential. As explored in *Chapter 4*, financial incentives drive both traffickers and those who enable them. If officials are paid competitive, consistent wages and have access to resources, they may be less inclined to risk their positions for a one-time bribe. Addressing systemic poverty and underfunding among law enforcement and border officials in source and transit countries is thus not merely a matter of human rights but a fundamental pillar of an effective anti-trafficking strategy.

As such, corruption along trafficking routes is a powerful enabler of human trafficking operations. From North African officials collaborating in Mediterranean crossings to American border agents turning a blind eye to trafficking on the southern border, the collusion of officials has become embedded in the global human trafficking network. Effective anti-trafficking policies must tackle these internal threats with the same rigour applied to external security measures, building systems where corruption does not open doors to exploitation but rather strengthens the global response against this pervasive crime.

Law Enforcement: Guardians or Collaborators?

Corruption within law enforcement fundamentally weakens the fight against human trafficking by creating a shielded environment where traffickers can operate with impunity. In source countries, particularly where trafficking is endemic, traffickers establish close relationships with local police forces. These alliances ensure that law enforcement officials, who should be dismantling trafficking operations, are instead protecting and enabling them. This collusion often manifests in two forms: passive acceptance, where officers look the other way, and active complicity, where police provide traffickers with protection in exchange for bribes or personal favours. This creates a systemic barrier that makes it nearly impossible to bring traffickers to justice without intervention from outside entities.

Entrenched Corruption in Source Countries: The Case of Southeast Asia and Latin America

In countries across Southeast Asia, Latin America, and parts of Eastern Europe, law enforcement corruption is so prevalent that traffickers operate openly, confident that police protection will shield them from prosecution. Southeast Asia, for example, has become a well-known trafficking hub where local law enforcement's involvement is not an isolated problem but an institutional one. Police officers in these regions frequently receive substantial payments from traffickers, enabling them to operate openly and move victims across borders or through cities without interference. These payments are not limited to cash bribes; traffickers may offer police access to illicit goods or even political favours, fostering a relationship that is mutually beneficial but morally bankrupt.

Latin America presents similar issues. With a history of political instability, economic challenges, and organised crime, parts of the region have seen law enforcement morph into an extension of the trafficking enterprise itself. Police officers, particularly those working in rural or impoverished areas, are often paid poorly and lack adequate resources. Traffickers exploit these vulnerabilities, offering financial incentives that far exceed official salaries. In return, police ensure that traffickers can move freely, evading checkpoints and avoiding arrests. In such environments, attempts to prosecute traffickers are frequently undermined, as local law enforcement officers are not only complicit but may actively obstruct investigations. This creates a paradox where the very authorities meant to combat trafficking become its facilitators.

High-Ranking Officials: Corruption at the Top

Corruption's impact is not limited to local law enforcement officers. High-ranking government and police officials are often implicated, wielding their influence to protect trafficking networks from disruption. These senior figures, driven by financial incentives or political pressures, may instruct their subordinates to overlook trafficking cases or, worse, may themselves be part of trafficking networks. When traffickers are brought to trial, high-ranking officials may exert pressure on judicial processes, ensuring that cases are dismissed, downgraded, or resolved with lenient sentences. In this way, the influence of powerful officials turns legal frameworks into tools that benefit traffickers, systematically dismantling any serious effort to punish them.

The result is a stark erosion of public trust in the legal system, particularly among victims. When victims know that high-ranking officials are complicit or that judicial outcomes are manipulated, they are less likely to seek help or report their exploitation. This eroded trust creates a vicious cycle in which traffickers feel secure enough to expand their operations, knowing that judicial recourse is unlikely. For trafficking victims, especially those who are undocumented or have precarious legal standing, this widespread corruption creates a formidable barrier. Even if they can escape or report their exploitation, they face a system skewed in favour of their oppressors.

Law Enforcement as Part of Trafficking Networks: The Role of Enforcers and Intimidators

Corrupt law enforcement officers, as explored in *Chapter 4* on organised crime networks, do not merely accept bribes to protect traffickers; some actively participate within trafficking networks themselves. In certain regions, police officers and military personnel are enlisted by trafficking groups to act as "enforcers," using their authority to intimidate victims, silence witnesses, and ensure that trafficking operations continue unimpeded. These enforcers leverage their official powers to frighten victims into compliance, creating an environment where victims are effectively trapped with no avenues for escape. Trafficking survivors have reported instances of being physically threatened by uniformed officers, who warn them of severe consequences if they attempt to escape or seek assistance.

In some cases, law enforcement involvement goes beyond intimidation and extends to the operational side of trafficking. Police officers may actively participate in the logistics of moving victims, using official vehicles to bypass checkpoints, transporting individuals between locations, or managing illegal "safe houses" where victims are hidden. These officers, aware of anti-trafficking operations and equipped with resources, may alert traffickers about upcoming raids or investigations. Such collusion dismantles the structural safeguards designed to protect trafficking victims and allows trafficking networks to flourish, insulated by their connections with law enforcement.

The Impact on Victims: Disillusionment and Isolation

For trafficking victims, particularly those who are undocumented or from economically disadvantaged backgrounds, the corruption of law enforcement creates a harrowing situation. Many trafficked individuals, fleeing conflict or extreme poverty, initially view law enforcement as their potential rescuers. However, the reality they encounter in source and destination countries can be profoundly disheartening. Once they realise that law enforcement officers are complicit or in some cases, actively involved in the trafficking cycle, any hope of rescue diminishes.

This disillusionment intensifies their sense of isolation, as traffickers exploit the fear instilled by corrupt police. Victims, who may already be traumatised and reluctant to trust others, become even less likely to reach out for help, knowing that the same officers who might rescue them are also paid to keep them compliant. This cycle of fear and isolation reinforces the trafficking network's control, as victims are led to believe that they are utterly alone in a hostile environment where every authority figure works in favour of their captors.

Eroding Community Trust and Perpetuating the Cycle

The endemic corruption within law enforcement has broader implications beyond individual trafficking cases; it erodes trust in governmental institutions at a societal level. When the public perceives that police officers and high-ranking officials are complicit in trafficking, it undermines confidence in the very foundations of justice and governance. Communities begin to see law enforcement as unreliable, prioritising financial gain over public safety, which discourages collective efforts to report or resist trafficking. This distrust allows traffickers to operate with even greater impunity, as community members may fear retaliation from law enforcement should they attempt to intervene or report suspicious activities.

This climate of distrust, along with the lack of accountability within law enforcement, perpetuates a cycle in which traffickers benefit from a degree of social licence. When public institutions fail to act in the interest of justice, traffickers are emboldened, and trafficking operations expand as public resistance wanes. In some regions, community leaders and activists face harassment or intimidation if they criticise law enforcement's complicity in trafficking, reinforcing a status quo where the traffickers and corrupted officials reinforce each other's power.

Toward Reform: Breaking the Cycle of Law Enforcement Corruption

To combat the role of corrupt law enforcement in trafficking, comprehensive reforms are essential. The first step is accountability instituting independent oversight committees that can investigate and prosecute law enforcement officers involved in trafficking networks. Enhanced whistleblower protections would encourage honest officers or community members to report corruption without fear of retaliation. To ensure that these reforms are impactful, international bodies could offer support by funding anti-corruption initiatives, training, and resources that strengthen local law enforcement in source countries.

Increasing pay and providing resources for law enforcement in source countries are also critical measures. As discussed earlier in *Chapter 4*, financial stability reduces vulnerability to bribery, creating a stronger sense of duty among officers. When law enforcement personnel receive fair wages and training in ethical conduct, they are more likely to resist traffickers' financial temptations and focus on dismantling trafficking operations. This shift, though gradual, could build the foundation for restoring public confidence in law enforcement and creating an environment where victims feel safe to seek help.

Ultimately, addressing law enforcement corruption requires a concerted effort, blending local reform with international cooperation to ensure that the very institutions meant to protect victims become allies in dismantling trafficking networks. Without addressing the internal decay within law enforcement, anti-trafficking efforts will continue to be undermined from within, trapping countless individuals in a cycle of exploitation sanctioned by those entrusted to serve and protect.

Corruption in the Judiciary and Government

Corruption within the judiciary and high levels of government poses an exceptionally insidious challenge in combating human trafficking. When government officials, legislators, or members of the judiciary themselves become entangled in trafficking networks or benefit financially from them, their influence weakens the rule of law, perpetuates trafficking, and undermines international cooperation. This high-level corruption poses a more profound threat than corruption within border or law enforcement agencies, as it systematically disrupts the structural and legal mechanisms intended to prevent and punish trafficking.

The Judicial System and Legislative Weakness

In numerous cases worldwide, corrupt government officials directly or indirectly dilute anti-trafficking laws. This may take the form of weakening sentencing requirements, creating loopholes in the legislation, or halting the passage of new laws that would otherwise empower law enforcement to pursue traffickers aggressively. For instance, in *Nigeria*, despite substantial anti-trafficking efforts, pervasive corruption has enabled traffickers to continue operations, often under the radar. Nigerian traffickers exploit the inability of the state to enforce existing anti-trafficking laws effectively, while political elites are alleged to either ignore the issue or, in some cases, benefit indirectly from the trafficking economy through political connections with traffickers. The United Nations Office on Drugs and Crime (UNODC) has identified political corruption in Nigeria as a significant barrier to anti-trafficking enforcement, underscoring how legislative and judicial complicity allows trafficking networks to thrive without consequence.

High-Level Governmental Involvement and Obstruction

In some cases, high-ranking officials not only obstruct anti-trafficking legislation but are complicit in trafficking activities or linked through political donations from trafficking syndicates. For example, in *Honduras*, a country that has struggled with corruption and organised crime, there have been cases where government officials were found to be connected to trafficking networks. In 2019, the former president of Honduras, Juan Orlando Hernández, was implicated in a U.S. drug-trafficking investigation involving links between drug traffickers and human traffickers, highlighting how corruption at the highest levels of government can provide cover for trafficking activities and render anti-trafficking efforts futile. Corruption in high offices erodes both national and international trust in Honduras's commitment to addressing trafficking, ultimately obstructing any progress that could be made by domestic or international actors.

In *Southeast Asia*, corruption in the judiciary and government similarly undermines anti-trafficking efforts. A notable example is *Thailand*, where anti-trafficking initiatives are frequently hindered by officials who either accept bribes or hold political interests in businesses that rely on forced labour. The 2015 exposure of human trafficking in Thai fishing industries, where enslaved workers were held on fishing vessels and worked without pay, was linked to systemic corruption that extended to government officials. Following international pressure, Thai authorities made several arrests; however, investigations revealed that high-ranking officials had been complicit or had turned a blind eye to trafficking activities, underscoring how government corruption perpetuates trafficking cycles. This case highlights that, while laws may exist on paper, they are effectively nullified by governmental complicity and reluctance to enforce them.

The Undermining of International Anti-Trafficking Frameworks

The Palermo Protocol, established as part of the United Nations' effort to prevent, suppress, and punish human trafficking, serves as the primary international framework to guide nations in their anti-trafficking efforts. While the majority of nations are signatories, corruption in the judiciary and government critically weakens the protocol's intended impact. *India*, for example, has ratified the Palermo Protocol and possesses stringent anti-trafficking laws. Yet, enforcement remains inconsistent, and cases frequently stagnate in the court system, often due to the influence of traffickers on judicial officers or public prosecutors. In several regions of India, traffickers are politically connected, which helps them escape conviction. Reports have shown that traffickers use their connections with local officials to avoid arrests, receive warnings about raids, or secure lenient sentencing when cases do reach the courts.

Another country struggling with the implementation of the Palermo Protocol due to entrenched corruption is *Cambodia*. Although Cambodia's laws align with the protocol, traffickers and their affiliates can still operate openly due to judicial corruption. Traffickers routinely bribe court officials, who in turn dismiss cases, reduce charges, or impose minimal penalties. The U.S. Department of State has noted that Cambodian officials have been directly involved in human trafficking operations or have obstructed investigations to shield influential traffickers. This undermines Cambodia's adherence to the Palermo Protocol, as laws that exist solely on paper fail to protect victims or deter traffickers.

Corruption in Legislative Bodies: Loopholes and Legislative Stagnation

In some countries, traffickers exploit legislative corruption to delay or prevent the passage of anti-trafficking laws. For instance, *Lebanon*, while under international pressure to strengthen its anti-trafficking legislation, has faced delays due to lobbying by political elites who are reportedly involved in industries that benefit from forced labour. In this environment, traffickers rely on legislative stagnation to continue their operations without the risk of enhanced penalties or broader law enforcement powers being enacted against them. Legislative bodies influenced by trafficking syndicates can also introduce ambiguities or loopholes within laws that allow traffickers to escape prosecution on technicalities, nullifying the impact of legislative measures designed to prevent trafficking.

The Need for International Oversight and Collaboration

In such environments, the only viable solutions often lie in external intervention and international collaboration. International monitoring bodies, such as the UNODC and Interpol, have worked alongside non-governmental organisations to expose instances of judicial and governmental corruption, placing pressure on countries to reform their systems. However, this approach requires the support of political leaders genuinely committed to change. For instance, *the Philippines* has made strides in recent years to combat trafficking, implementing reforms in cooperation with the U.S. and other international partners. Despite its success, the programme's effectiveness is threatened by periodic reports of governmental corruption, suggesting that sustained external pressure is necessary to ensure that judicial and governmental corruption does not re-emerge as a barrier to enforcement.

In conclusion, corruption within the judiciary and high-ranking government officials fundamentally weakens national and international anti-trafficking efforts. This systemic issue not only enables traffickers but actively undermines the Palermo Protocol and similar frameworks, rendering them powerless in the face of entrenched collusion and bribery. Addressing this form of corruption requires both internal reform and sustained international oversight to dismantle the protective barriers that traffickers rely on to operate with impunity.

Undermining Victims' Rights and Legal Protections

Corruption in anti-trafficking enforcement not only facilitates the criminal networks involved in human trafficking but also systematically erodes the rights and protections of trafficking victims. When victims of trafficking are denied their legal protections, they endure further suffering under state institutions that, in theory, should be protecting them. This corruption compounds the trauma of trafficking, as victims are criminalised, silenced, and discouraged from seeking justice.

Victims as Criminals

In numerous cases, victims of trafficking are treated as criminals rather than as individuals in need of protection, particularly in countries where corruption in law enforcement is rampant. Many trafficking victims are undocumented immigrants who, upon escape or detainment, are vulnerable to prosecution rather than protection. In such instances, corrupt officials may exploit these individuals' legal vulnerability, arresting and detaining them without affording them the protections they are entitled to under international law, such as those outlined in the United Nations Palermo Protocol.

In Southeast Asia, for example, migrant women trafficked for sexual exploitation are often arrested for prostitution or deported as illegal immigrants. In Thailand, despite progressive anti-trafficking legislation, it has been documented that law enforcement sometimes arrests and jails trafficked individuals, particularly undocumented immigrants, as a method of deterrence. Victims, in such environments, are fearful of the very authorities who should offer them protection and are often unaware of their legal rights. Corrupt officers may take advantage of this ignorance to expedite deportations or detain victims as a means of keeping trafficking cases out of court.

Destruction of Evidence and Obstruction of Justice

Corrupt law enforcement officials, often under the influence of traffickers' bribes, may go so far as to actively obstruct justice by destroying evidence, manipulating investigations, or intimidating victims. This issue is particularly evident in countries where law enforcement and judicial systems are vulnerable to bribery or political influence. In Mexico, for example, NGOs have documented cases where law enforcement officers destroy critical evidence, such as confiscated documents or recorded testimonies, which could be used to prosecute traffickers. These actions sabotage the judicial process and ultimately shield traffickers from prosecution, leaving victims with no legal recourse or recognition as trafficked individuals. Victims, fearing potential repercussions and the futility of a corrupt legal system, are often left with no option but to endure their exploitation in silence.

In countries such as Nigeria, where trafficking is a persistent issue, traffickers often have close ties with police officers who are willing to ensure that cases never reach court. Reports have highlighted cases in which police officers accept bribes to either dismiss cases or intimidate victims and witnesses into withdrawing their testimonies. This level of corruption fundamentally degrades the legal protections for trafficking victims, silencing their voices and allowing traffickers to operate without fear of legal consequences.

Deportation, Detention, and the Failure to Recognise Victims

A particularly egregious consequence of corruption is the deportation or detention of victims without due consideration of their trafficking status. Trafficking victims, especially those from impoverished backgrounds or who are undocumented, are at the mercy of corrupt officials who may expedite deportations for financial gain. In Europe, this has been observed in certain cases involving undocumented immigrants trafficked from North Africa and Eastern Europe. For instance, in Italy, trafficking victims, particularly those exploited in forced labour or sexual exploitation, are frequently deported without a thorough investigation into their background or recognition of their victim status. Officials, motivated by bribes or quotas to reduce the undocumented population, treat trafficking cases as mere immigration violations, denying victims both justice and refuge.

This practice not only violates international protocols, such as the Palermo Protocol but also deprives victims of basic human rights. Victims of trafficking, rather than being offered support, are sent back to regions where they face the same or even worse conditions, while traffickers remain unchallenged, their criminal activities undeterred by legal repercussions.

Challenges for NGOs and International Organisations

Non-governmental organisations (NGOs) and international organisations play a crucial role in supporting and protecting trafficking victims, offering legal aid, shelter, and avenues for rehabilitation. However, in countries with high levels of corruption, these organisations face enormous challenges in their mission. Corrupt officials may restrict NGOs' operations, impose bureaucratic obstacles, or intimidate staff members, particularly when these organisations expose local government complicity in trafficking or attempt to provide legal support for victims.

For example, in Cambodia, where trafficking is deeply entrenched, some NGOs face pressure from local officials who limit their ability to investigate trafficking incidents or assist victims. The Cambodian government has been criticised for obstructing the work of organisations that advocate for trafficking victims, especially when cases involve local authorities. NGOs, aware of the potential dangers, may be forced to curb their advocacy or limit their efforts to avoid conflicts with corrupt officials. Such obstruction not only hampers their ability to provide critical services to victims but also discourages victims from coming forward, knowing that the organisations tasked with helping them are unable to operate without restrictions.

Retaliation Against Victims and Witnesses

Victims are often reluctant to testify against their traffickers due to the very real risk of retaliation from corrupt officials. This fear is particularly strong in source countries where trafficking networks are embedded within communities and maintain close ties with law enforcement. For instance, in Latin American countries such as Honduras, where both human trafficking and corruption are endemic, victims often fear reprisal not only from traffickers but also from local officials aligned with them. Victims who do attempt to testify or seek legal redress may find themselves, or their families, targeted by corrupt officials, with threats of violence or deportation. The intimidation of witnesses in this way essentially silences victims, preventing them from seeking justice or breaking free from the cycle of exploitation.

Even in countries with stronger legal protections for trafficking victims, such as the United States, cases of retaliation against victims have been documented. Trafficking victims are often undocumented and fear that any attempt to testify may result in deportation, especially if they encounter officials unsympathetic to their status. Although protections are theoretically in place, corruption or bias within immigration enforcement can mean that victims' testimonies lead to negative consequences for them, reducing the likelihood that traffickers will face justice.

Corruption within law enforcement, judicial systems, and government structures undermines the entire framework of anti-trafficking protections, stripping victims of their rights and protections. When victims are treated as criminals, detained, deported, or silenced, traffickers gain further impunity, allowing trafficking networks to thrive without interference. NGOs and international organisations, though crucial in the fight against trafficking, face systemic obstruction in corrupt environments, limiting their capacity to aid victims. The fear of retaliation effectively silences victims and discourages witness cooperation, perpetuating the cycle of trafficking and exploitation. Comprehensive anti-corruption reforms, transparency in law enforcement, and international pressure are essential if these systemic barriers are to be dismantled and true protections for trafficking victims are to be realised.

Conclusion: Addressing the Root of the Problem

In examining the role of corruption in human trafficking, it becomes clear that without tackling the systemic corruption embedded within governance and law enforcement structures, efforts to combat trafficking will remain ineffective. Corruption allows traffickers to operate with impunity, undermining both national and international anti-trafficking measures.

It is not enough to simply strengthen laws or increase border security; the very institutions tasked with upholding these laws must also be purged of corruption. This requires a multi-faceted approach, combining legal reform, international cooperation, and rigorous oversight of law enforcement and government officials. Only by addressing these issues can we hope to dismantle the networks that profit from human suffering and bring about meaningful change in the fight against human trafficking.

As I will explore further in the subsequent chapters, solutions do exist. But they require a commitment from governments, organisations, and individuals to confront the uncomfortable truth that corruption is not just a by-product of trafficking it is a central pillar holding up the entire structure. Only by removing this pillar can we begin to dismantle the trafficking networks that have enslaved millions around the world.

Chapter 6: The Digital Age: How Technology Fuels Human Trafficking

As we navigate the complexities of human trafficking in this modern era, it becomes apparent that technology is not merely a tool of convenience or connection; it is, tragically, an enabler of exploitation. Traffickers, both seasoned and emerging, are wielding the power of the internet, social media, and encrypted communication with chilling efficiency to recruit, exploit, and control their victims. The rise of the "dark web" has transformed human trafficking into a global digital enterprise, providing traffickers with a shadowy marketplace where people are reduced to commodities. To truly understand the scale and sophistication of trafficking in the digital age, we must delve deeply into the mechanisms traffickers use, the anonymity they thrive on, and the near-invisible networks they form within the depths of cyberspace.

This chapter will expand upon previous explorations of trafficking's roots, its routes, and the machinery driving it, as I discussed in Chapters 1 to 5. Where Chapters 2 and 4 laid bare the tangible networks and physical routes through which traffickers operate, here we move into the intangible, hidden realm that bolsters their operations. I will also draw upon insights from Chapter 5, where we saw how corruption and a lack of governance create fertile ground for these criminal activities. Indeed, technology is not only a tool for traffickers but also a means of circumventing both legal and ethical barriers. As we shall see, the very aspects of technology that facilitate global connectivity and financial innovation also lend themselves to the rapid, covert, and widespread operations that make human trafficking a colossal challenge in the digital age.

The Role of the Internet in Recruitment and Exploitation

The internet has indeed transformed recruitment methods for human traffickers, allowing them to tap into platforms built for connection and self-expression. Through social media, online dating apps, job boards, and even gaming sites, traffickers exploit the reach, anonymity, and vast data available online. This expansive reach means they can contact vulnerable individuals on a scale that would have been unthinkable before the digital era. Their tactics are honed with precision to blend seamlessly into these online ecosystems, with recruiters displaying a nuanced understanding of technology, social media algorithms, and cultural trends to deceive and manipulate victims. To understand the mechanics of this exploitation, it is essential to explore how traffickers deploy social engineering, data manipulation, and psychological grooming to lure victims into situations of exploitation and control.

Leveraging Algorithms and Targeted Advertising

Social media platforms and dating apps rely on sophisticated algorithms designed to deliver personalised content and recommendations, matching users with profiles, advertisements, and posts that align with their interests, location, and browsing history. Traffickers exploit these algorithms by tailoring profiles, posts, and advertisements that appeal directly to specific demographics they deem vulnerable such as young individuals from economically disadvantaged regions, people openly seeking employment opportunities, or those expressing discontent with their current circumstances. By targeting such individuals, traffickers can increase the likelihood of interaction, knowing that the algorithm will continue to push their fake profiles or job advertisements to the forefront of these users' feeds.

These traffickers often create multiple profiles, each appealing to a different type of vulnerable person. For example, on a job board, they may post as an international recruiter with connections to high-paying jobs abroad, while on dating platforms, they pose as potential romantic partners. With platforms offering insights into user interests, location, and activity, traffickers can tailor their outreach to maximise engagement. In some cases, they even pay for advertisements, disguising exploitative offers as legitimate employment or dating opportunities, allowing them to reach thousands or even millions of potential victims across geographical boundaries.

Fake Profiles, Grooming, and Psychological Manipulation

A common tactic traffickers use on social media and dating platforms is creating fake profiles that seem approachable, often posing as trustworthy professionals, romantic prospects, or successful expatriates. These profiles are carefully crafted, with images stolen from real users or stock photo sites, biographies that resonate with the target audience, and posts that portray a life of success, stability, or adventure. The goal is to create an illusion that these accounts represent real people with the means to offer companionship, work, or assistance to those looking for a fresh start.

Once contact is made, traffickers utilise grooming techniques that rely heavily on psychological manipulation, building a rapport and gaining trust over days, weeks, or even months. Initially, the trafficker presents themselves as a compassionate, understanding friend or partner, offering empathy and support to the target's expressed struggles. This process, often termed "love-bombing" in romantic grooming cases, involves showering the victim with attention, compliments, and promises of a better future. Traffickers may also probe for personal information, asking questions about family, financial struggles, or dreams, which they later use to manipulate and coerce their victims.

In cases where the trafficker poses as a job recruiter, the approach is more professional but equally deceptive. They may request CVs, conduct fake interviews, or provide references all designed to lend credibility to the scam. The promised "opportunity" is painted in broad strokes, with vague details that appeal to the victim's aspirations while avoiding specifics that might raise suspicions. Victims are often lured by promises of high-paying jobs abroad, in industries such as hospitality, domestic work, or modelling, where their skills will purportedly be appreciated and rewarded. By the time any suspicion arises, many victims are already emotionally invested or financially committed, making it challenging to back out.

Cultural and Demographic Tailoring

Traffickers adapt their approaches to reflect the cultural backgrounds, languages, and social norms of the demographic they are targeting. This cultural tailoring not only makes the outreach seem genuine but also enhances the manipulative impact. For example, traffickers targeting individuals from certain Southeast Asian or African countries might promise stable work abroad in fields familiar to those regions, such as domestic work, agriculture, or construction, where workers often face economic hardship. Similarly, traffickers targeting young women from Eastern Europe may use the glamour of Western modelling opportunities or "au pair" placements to entice their victims.

Language manipulation is also a powerful tool, especially when traffickers operate across linguistic barriers. They use culturally resonant slang, references to local customs, or even portray certain values (e.g., family support, a chance for social mobility) to resonate with victims on a personal level. Their messages are often crafted to match the dialect, idioms, and online trends familiar to the target demographic, making the trafficker's persona appear more relatable and, therefore, more trustworthy.

The Role of Visual and Content Manipulation

In addition to linguistic tactics, traffickers use visual manipulation to bolster their deception. Fake profiles often feature a curated selection of photos that tell a carefully crafted story aligned with the persona traffickers wish to portray. A trafficker posing as a romantic partner might include images of travel, high-status gatherings, or a "well-rounded" lifestyle, while a job recruiter may share images of corporate environments or work sites where the prospective job is purported to take place. The objective is to create an illusion that aligns with the victim's aspirations, reinforcing the sense that the trafficker can fulfil the promises they are making.

On certain platforms, traffickers use "status symbols" to make their profiles more appealing to individuals from lower socio-economic backgrounds. For instance, a photo of a luxurious hotel, high-end electronics, or branded clothing can signal financial stability and prosperity to a target who may be struggling economically. The visual presentation often supports a narrative that the trafficker is trustworthy, well-connected, and capable of providing the lifestyle they are advertising.

Isolation and Control: Manipulation of Social and Digital Connections

Social media platforms not only facilitate initial contact but also allow traffickers to isolate their victims by encouraging secrecy or discouraging connections outside the trafficker-victim relationship. A trafficker may initially build trust by emphasising the unique connection they share with the victim, urging them to keep their relationship private "for their safety" or to avoid "jealousy" from friends or family. Once isolated, traffickers can tighten their grip, increasing control over the victim's communication and online interactions.

Some traffickers demand access to a victim's social media accounts, purportedly to "protect" them, but in reality, this access allows them to monitor or even restrict communication with others. This form of digital isolation mirrors the physical isolation that traffickers traditionally use to assert dominance and restrict a victim's access to outside help. It is not uncommon for traffickers to threaten to share compromising information they may have coerced from victims such as intimate photos or details of their family creating a psychological prison where the victim feels unable to break free.

Exploiting Real-Time Data and Geolocation

Advanced features on social media, like location sharing or activity status indicators, can also be exploited by traffickers to monitor a victim's movements and routine behaviours. While ostensibly harmless to everyday users, real-time location tracking can give traffickers a way to observe and potentially control a victim's movements, either by establishing a pattern to understand the best time to interact or by knowing when a victim is geographically near a staging point for abduction or exploitation.

For instance, traffickers using platforms with geolocation features may encourage victims to "check-in" at various locations under the guise of sharing their experiences, all while gathering data to assess vulnerability or track movement. Real-time data from platforms that track when users are online (such as "last seen" features) can also allow traffickers to apply pressure or re-engage victims with precisely timed messages, creating a sense of omnipresence that fosters dependency and submission.

In summary, the internet has expanded the arsenal of methods traffickers use to recruit, control, and exploit victims. They masterfully leverage algorithms, social engineering, and psychological manipulation to create an environment in which victims feel ensnared, isolated, and ultimately powerless. As the internet continues to evolve, so too will traffickers' strategies, underscoring the urgent need for effective countermeasures to disrupt these digital pathways to exploitation.

The Dark Web: A Marketplace for Human Trafficking

The dark web, that hidden part of the internet requiring special browsers to access, has become an insidious marketplace where traffickers can operate with relative impunity. Unlike the visible web, the dark web is characterised by anonymity and encrypted transactions, creating a perfect breeding ground for illicit trade, including human trafficking. It is here that traffickers sell individuals as commodities, reducing human beings to nothing more than transactions to be made for profit.

Operating beyond the reach of conventional search engines and law enforcement, the dark web functions like an underground bazaar. Traffickers can advertise their "products" in disturbing detail, complete with images, descriptions, and even pricing schemes, catering to those willing to purchase people for forced labour or sexual exploitation. Transactions are often conducted in cryptocurrencies, making the trade even more elusive. Cryptocurrency, with its decentralised and often anonymous nature, facilitates these illegal dealings while complicating the efforts of law enforcement agencies to track the flow of funds.

In previous chapters, we explored the physical routes traffickers use to move victims from source to destination countries. The dark web serves as an equivalent digital route, linking buyers and sellers across continents in a faceless, borderless exchange. However, unlike traditional trafficking routes, which can be mapped and intercepted, the dark web remains difficult to surveil and nearly impossible to police. This marketplace operates in a state of constant flux, with websites disappearing and reappearing, a tactic designed to evade detection by authorities. Law enforcement agencies find themselves chasing a constantly shifting target, hindered by the technical barriers that protect this digital underworld.

Encrypted Communication and Evading Detection

Encrypted communication tools have revolutionised the operational landscape for traffickers, providing a shield that conceals the entirety of their illicit activities. Platforms like WhatsApp, Signal, and Telegram, with their end-to-end encryption, mean that messages are only readable on the devices of the sender and receiver, making interception by third parties nearly impossible. This encryption method operates in a way that even the platform hosting the communication cannot decrypt messages, essentially rendering communications invisible to outside scrutiny, including law enforcement. With such impenetrable barriers, traffickers can coordinate highly complex, multi-national operations, maintaining real-time communication without the risk of exposure that once characterised their activities.

Enhancing Organised Networks with Encrypted Messaging

As detailed in Chapter 4, trafficking networks rely on a hierarchy of roles, from recruiters and transporters to enforcers and handlers, who collectively execute the various stages of exploitation. Encrypted messaging strengthens this hierarchy by allowing traffickers to communicate instantly, reliably, and securely across borders. A recruiter based in Southeast Asia can, for instance, relay precise instructions to transporters in Europe or handlers in North America, adjusting logistical plans on the fly to evade authorities. This real-time adaptability means that traffickers can respond immediately to any challenges, whether they arise from law enforcement interference, logistical delays, or even victims' resistance.

Encrypted communication tools have also redefined the way traffickers approach geographical challenges. With end-to-end encryption, trafficking operations do not need to rely on a centralised location or physical meeting points to disseminate plans or exchange sensitive information. Operations can be broken down into smaller, independent cells, with each cell leader only needing to communicate with a single point in the chain, reducing the chance of exposure. This decentralisation is significant because even if law enforcement were to intercept or disrupt one part of the chain, the remainder of the network can continue to function autonomously, reducing the impact of such breaches.

Cross-Border Coordination and Global Expansion

The proliferation of encrypted messaging tools has also emboldened traffickers to operate beyond traditional borders, seamlessly coordinating activities between source, transit, and destination countries. For instance, a trafficking ring may orchestrate the recruitment of victims in Central America, facilitate their smuggling through complex routes in Mexico, and arrange for their "placement" in exploitative conditions within the United States all through encrypted messages exchanged between contacts in each country.

This level of coordination means that traffickers can rely on highly efficient logistics, with each participant in the trafficking network receiving detailed, location-specific instructions without ever meeting face-to-face. Such digital anonymity not only reduces operational costs but also helps traffickers expand into new territories with relative ease. This expansion is often achieved through temporary alliances with other criminal networks or freelancers, with encrypted messaging serving as the backbone of communication and negotiation between these loosely connected entities.

The effect is an interconnected web of traffickers who may operate independently yet communicate fluidly, strengthening the overall network's resilience to law enforcement efforts. By embracing encrypted communication, traffickers have created what is effectively a borderless operation, constantly in motion, with only digital fingerprints left as evidence fingerprints that are virtually indecipherable due to the layers of encryption.

Digital Control and Psychological Manipulation of Victims

Encrypted messaging also plays a crucial role in exerting psychological control over victims, allowing traffickers to reinforce threats and commands remotely. Even after victims are moved to a destination country, traffickers can maintain control over them by sending explicit instructions and threats through encrypted messages, often warning of harm to their families or of severe penalties if they attempt to escape. This form of remote control fosters a state of constant surveillance and anxiety in victims, who feel as if their trafficker's presence looms over them despite the physical distance.

The use of encrypted communication for such psychological manipulation ensures that traffickers can maintain a strong grip on victims without needing to resort to physical confinement, relying instead on fear and digital monitoring. This tactic is especially prevalent in sex trafficking and forced labour cases, where victims might have limited freedom of movement but remain psychologically imprisoned. Furthermore, traffickers may use these channels to extract additional value from victims by forcing them to send periodic photos or videos as proof of compliance, keeping them psychologically tethered to their abusers.

Law Enforcement Challenges: The Double-Edged Sword of Encryption

The resilience of encrypted communication presents one of the most formidable challenges to anti-trafficking efforts. While encryption is a cornerstone of privacy rights in democratic societies, it also creates significant barriers for law enforcement agencies attempting to investigate and dismantle trafficking rings. Even when authorities obtain legal warrants, the technical barriers posed by encryption often mean they can only access metadata such as message timestamps and user contact lists but not the content of the messages themselves.

The implications of this digital opacity are profound. For example, a trafficker's encrypted conversation with a recruiter or enforcer might be visible as a data point but completely shielded in terms of content. Consequently, law enforcement loses vital intelligence that could otherwise confirm recruitment tactics, identify accomplices, or uncover the locations of trafficked individuals. The legal and ethical conundrum becomes even more complex in cases where traffickers exploit platforms that integrate "self-destructing" messages or timed erasure features, which delete messages after a specified period, leaving no trace even if a device is later accessed.

Emerging Technology: The Evolution of Encrypted Communication

Adding to the complexity, traffickers are increasingly moving beyond standard messaging apps and adopting newer technologies with advanced encryption features, such as decentralised applications and anonymous, blockchain-based messaging platforms. These platforms go beyond traditional end-to-end encryption, utilising blockchain to decentralise the storage and transfer of messages, rendering even the metadata difficult to trace.

In some cases, traffickers use the dark web to communicate on platforms specifically designed for anonymity, such as Tor-based email services or encrypted forums that require multiple layers of authentication. These tools offer additional protections by masking IP addresses and preventing any form of centralised tracking, making it extremely difficult for law enforcement to detect communication channels, let alone intercept messages. Such advancements give traffickers an added layer of security, enabling them to feel increasingly emboldened in expanding operations and evading capture.

Legal and Ethical Dilemmas in Combating Encrypted Communications

The encrypted communications challenge poses not only technical but also significant legal and ethical dilemmas. Privacy advocates argue that end-to-end encryption is fundamental to protecting the rights of individuals against unwarranted surveillance. However, traffickers have weaponised these protections to operate with impunity, exploiting legal and technological limitations that prevent law enforcement from monitoring their communications.

The balancing act between privacy rights and the need to prevent serious crimes like human trafficking has sparked intense debate and calls for "backdoors" in encryption systems, whereby law enforcement could access encrypted messages under certain conditions. Such proposals, however, are fraught with risks, as they could potentially compromise the security of millions of innocent users and open the door to abuses by both government and non-state actors. This legal impasse has, thus far, left authorities grappling with inadequate tools to access and interpret traffickers' communications, while traffickers continue to exploit the anonymity that encryption affords.

Towards a Solution: Bridging Privacy and Security in Anti-Trafficking Efforts

Addressing the encrypted communications conundrum will require innovative approaches that balance individual privacy with the need for effective anti-trafficking interventions. Solutions could include the development of more sophisticated AI and machine learning tools that can analyse metadata patterns to detect trafficking networks without needing direct access to message content. Another potential avenue is the establishment of international cooperation frameworks, which allow for cross-border sharing of metadata and suspect profiles, helping to link data points across jurisdictions and uncover larger trafficking patterns.

Furthermore, social media and messaging platforms could play a more proactive role by implementing algorithms that detect and flag suspicious activity patterns, such as the rapid formation of group chats with known trafficking signals or the creation of multiple accounts under single device IDs. By working collaboratively with law enforcement, technology companies could contribute to curbing traffickers' reliance on these encrypted spaces without sacrificing privacy rights wholesale.

Encrypted communication tools remain both a safeguard for individual privacy and a shield for traffickers, but they need not be an insurmountable obstacle. By leveraging technological, legal, and policy-oriented strategies, it may be possible to preserve the integrity of private communications while simultaneously taking significant strides towards dismantling the digital channels that human traffickers exploit so mercilessly.

Cryptocurrencies: The Financial Fuel of the Trafficking Trade

Cryptocurrencies have emerged as an indispensable asset for human traffickers, enabling them to operate with unprecedented financial anonymity. Traditionally, traffickers faced significant obstacles in moving and laundering money, as banks and financial institutions are required by law to monitor transactions and report any suspicious activity. With cryptocurrencies like Bitcoin, however, traffickers gain direct access to a decentralised financial network that operates largely outside the regulatory purview of banks or government agencies, allowing them to transfer and access funds instantly and with minimal oversight. This digital financial independence has transformed the human trafficking industry, enhancing traffickers' ability to conceal transactions and reinvest illicit gains back into the business, often undetected.

The Decentralised Nature of Cryptocurrencies and Blockchain

At the heart of cryptocurrency's appeal to traffickers is its decentralised structure. Unlike traditional currencies, which are issued and regulated by central banks, cryptocurrencies operate on a peer-to-peer network built upon blockchain technology. The blockchain is essentially a public ledger of all transactions, spread across countless computers worldwide. This decentralisation means that no single authority controls the currency or has full visibility into its transactions, a quality that traffickers exploit to avoid detection.

Blockchain transactions are generally pseudonymous; while each transaction is recorded, it is identified by a wallet address rather than a user's identity. In practice, this pseudonymity means that the identities of those behind the transactions can be extremely difficult to trace. To transfer money, traffickers only need a recipient's wallet address, which consists of a series of letters and numbers unlinked to a physical location or identity. As long as traffickers can keep their real-world identities separate from their digital wallets, they can move substantial sums without triggering the usual anti-money laundering (AML) flags that are common in traditional finance.

Advantages of Cryptocurrencies for Cross-Border Transactions

For traffickers, the decentralised and cross-border nature of cryptocurrencies makes them ideal for transferring funds across jurisdictions instantly. Unlike international bank transfers, which can take days and require complex verification steps, cryptocurrency transactions are near-instantaneous and only depend on network confirmation. This speed enables traffickers to fund their operations or disburse payments to accomplices across the globe with minimal delay. Additionally, because cryptocurrencies operate outside the traditional banking system, these transfers avoid regulatory checks and international currency controls, providing traffickers with an untraceable, borderless means of moving money.

As trafficking operations often span multiple countries, the ability to transfer funds quickly and anonymously is critical. For example, a trafficker may transfer Bitcoin to pay a recruiter in one country, a transporter in another, and a handler in yet another, all without alerting authorities. Furthermore, because cryptocurrencies are not tied to any single currency system, traffickers are free from concerns over currency conversion fees or exchange rate fluctuations, which can cut into their profits when using traditional financial methods.

Cryptocurrency as a Tool for Laundering Profits

Beyond facilitating cross-border transfers, cryptocurrencies are also instrumental in laundering proceeds. In the past, traffickers faced significant barriers when attempting to launder large sums, as banks and financial institutions are vigilant about reporting unusual transactions. Cryptocurrencies, however, allow traffickers to obscure the origins of their profits through methods such as "mixing" or "tumbling." These techniques involve pooling funds from multiple wallets and redistributing them in a way that obscures the source, breaking the clear trail of transactions visible on the blockchain.

For example, a trafficker may use a Bitcoin mixing service, which combines multiple Bitcoin transactions and redistributes them to various wallets, effectively "washing" the coins so that they appear to originate from multiple sources rather than a single illegal operation. Additionally, some traffickers employ "chain hopping," a process by which they convert one cryptocurrency into another such as from Bitcoin to Monero or Zcash, both of which are known for their enhanced privacy features. Chain hopping obscures the transaction history, as each conversion complicates the tracing efforts of authorities, especially when privacy-focused coins are involved.

Privacy-Focused Cryptocurrencies and Increased Anonymity

While Bitcoin and Ethereum are relatively transparent, new privacy-focused cryptocurrencies like Monero, Zcash, and Dash have added another layer of complexity to law enforcement's efforts. These cryptocurrencies are designed to conceal not only the parties involved but also the amounts and frequencies of transactions, using advanced encryption methods that make them nearly impossible to track. Monero, for example, employs ring signatures and stealth addresses, which allow for completely anonymous transactions. This technology prevents anyone from determining which wallet belongs to whom or how much is transferred, creating a virtually untraceable money trail.

These privacy features have made Monero and similar coins highly attractive to traffickers. Because these cryptocurrencies were created to offer users an additional layer of financial privacy, traffickers can use them to safeguard their operations against detection. For instance, a trafficking network might receive payments in Monero and convert them into Bitcoin or another currency only when they are ready to access the funds, thus "cleansing" the transaction history and providing yet another barrier for law enforcement to cross.

Funding Expansion and Recruitment with Cryptocurrency Proceeds

As explored in Chapter 5, financial gain remains one of the most powerful drivers of human trafficking. Cryptocurrency not only enables traffickers to protect these profits but also provides them with the flexibility to reinvest in their operations. Using digital currency, traffickers can anonymously fund the recruitment of new victims, pay for transportation routes, and bribe officials to ensure safe passage. These funds also support the technology infrastructure that traffickers increasingly rely upon, including secure communication tools, encrypted storage for sensitive data, and even online advertisements to lure new victims, as explored in previous chapters.

Cryptocurrencies offer traffickers a safe repository for their earnings, allowing them to accumulate capital without the risk of having it seized by authorities. Traditional methods of wealth storage, such as bank accounts, real estate, or luxury assets, carry a high risk of detection and seizure, especially in jurisdictions with robust anti-trafficking laws. Cryptocurrencies, however, are stored in digital wallets protected by complex cryptographic keys, making them nearly impossible to seize without the wallet owner's cooperation.

This hidden digital capital also enables traffickers to maintain operational resilience. If one route or group within the network is compromised, traffickers can swiftly redirect resources to other parts of the operation, minimising disruption and avoiding financial losses. In this way, cryptocurrencies do not just support the day-to-day operations of trafficking rings but actively contribute to their growth and sustainability.

Challenges for Law Enforcement and Regulatory Bodies

The decentralised, anonymous nature of cryptocurrencies presents a substantial hurdle for law enforcement. Traditional AML mechanisms, such as transaction reporting, account monitoring, and customer identification, are ineffective within the world of cryptocurrency. Law enforcement agencies face the added challenge of international jurisdiction; while a single bank transfer can often be scrutinised within a nation's borders, a cryptocurrency transaction spans multiple countries and is often inaccessible to any single authority.

Furthermore, the emergence of decentralised exchanges (DEXs), which operate without a central authority, has made it even more difficult for regulators to intervene. DEXs allow users to trade cryptocurrencies without requiring personal identification, enabling traffickers to convert and transfer their illicit earnings undetected. By leveraging DEXs, traffickers avoid the centralised exchanges, which are increasingly required to comply with Know Your Customer (KYC) and AML regulations. Many traffickers deliberately avoid regulated exchanges and choose to work within peer-to-peer networks and decentralised systems, shielding themselves from oversight.

Even in cases where law enforcement can track down the wallets used by traffickers, the decentralised nature of blockchain technology complicates the process of asset seizure. Unlike bank accounts or physical assets, digital wallets do not have physical locations and cannot be "frozen" in the traditional sense. Law enforcement would need private keys to access these wallets, and without these, there is little recourse for authorities to disrupt traffickers' access to funds.

The Double-Edged Sword of Cryptocurrency: The Balance of Innovation and Crime Prevention

Cryptocurrencies have undeniably transformed many aspects of modern finance, offering people across the globe unprecedented financial freedom and privacy. However, as this chapter illustrates, these same qualities can be weaponised by traffickers to conduct and expand their operations. The very decentralisation and privacy that make cryptocurrencies appealing to the general public also allow traffickers to operate beyond the reach of law enforcement.

In response, some governments and regulatory bodies are exploring ways to address this gap. Proposals for increased regulation include compelling cryptocurrency exchanges to implement more stringent KYC measures and requiring greater cooperation with international law enforcement. In some cases, law enforcement agencies are using blockchain analysis tools and artificial intelligence to track and flag suspicious cryptocurrency activity, though these efforts are still in their infancy and often lag behind traffickers' evolving strategies.

This regulatory balancing act is further complicated by the fact that privacy rights must also be protected. The need for a regulatory framework that disrupts traffickers without infringing on individual freedoms represents an ongoing challenge. At present, the reach of law enforcement and regulatory bodies into the world of cryptocurrency remains limited, leaving traffickers with a financial network that is as secure as it is exploitable.

As cryptocurrencies continue to evolve, they will likely remain a double-edged sword in the fight against human trafficking a tool of liberation for many and an instrument of exploitation for others.

Online Platforms and the Challenge of Regulation

The use of online platforms in technology-fuelled human trafficking presents a rapidly evolving challenge, with traffickers exploiting the unique structures of social media to recruit, advertise, and coordinate criminal activities with relative ease and impunity. **TikTok, for example, has emerged as a particularly insidious tool in this realm, as traffickers leverage its extensive reach, youthful user base, and highly visual format to target potential victims** and even recruit intermediaries, such as drivers and drug mules, through seemingly innocent content.

The Role of TikTok and Other Social Media in Recruitment and Coordination

Traffickers exploit TikTok's popularity among young people, a demographic often marked by higher susceptibility to manipulation, social pressure, and financial need. With the app's algorithm promoting content based on engagement patterns, traffickers can exploit trending hashtags or challenges to attract individuals who may be open to quick-money schemes. **For instance, traffickers use vague or coded language in videos, often cloaked as job opportunities or lifestyle enhancements, inviting interested viewers to "DM for details"** a common phrase implying that direct communication will reveal more about the offer. These messages target viewers struggling with economic hardships or looking for unconventional work, appealing to their desire for rapid income through high-paying but vague "driver" or "courier" roles.

Through TikTok, traffickers disguise these roles with enticing portrayals of fast money and minimal effort, often omitting the risks involved or the illegal nature of the tasks. Recruiters may craft engaging content showing individuals flaunting cash, luxury items, or freedom of movement, deliberately appealing to young viewers seeking an escape from limited local opportunities. This approach is especially effective among economically disadvantaged youth, who may see these visuals as a ticket out of hardship, unaware that they are potentially being groomed to transport illicit goods, traffic drugs, or move victims for trafficking networks. The conversational, informal nature of TikTok's user experience provides an ideal cover for traffickers, who adapt to the platform's stylistic norms to avoid suspicion.

Content Moderation Challenges on Social Media Platforms

Platforms like TikTok and Instagram face immense challenges in detecting and addressing trafficking-related content. **Moderation** algorithms are often unable to differentiate between legitimate content and material disguised to recruit or deceive potential victims, as traffickers frequently use coded language, symbols, or memes to communicate without triggering moderation filters. As a result, even when explicit keywords are flagged, traffickers can adjust their messaging to remain below detection thresholds, often with highly localised slang or emojis known only within certain communities.

Content moderators, while diligent, face overwhelming workloads, often struggling to review and remove illegal content in real-time. Unlike structured platforms (such as job boards with clearer reporting structures), TikTok is based on high-volume, rapid interactions where millions of videos are posted daily. The constant influx of content stretches the capacity of both human moderators and AI tools, and traffickers exploit this fast-paced environment to post brief, ephemeral content that can evade capture by being taken down before moderators flag it.

International Challenges in Regulating Online Platforms

The regulatory environment further complicates efforts to combat trafficking through these platforms. **Platforms like TikTok are multinational, with operations across jurisdictions that may not align on legal definitions, enforcement priorities, or penalties related to trafficking content.** A platform headquartered in the West, where regulations may strictly govern trafficking-related content, may still serve users in regions with less stringent trafficking laws or enforcement mechanisms. This discrepancy enables traffickers to operate from countries where digital oversight is minimal or cooperation with international law enforcement is limited.

International law enforcement agencies and regulatory bodies face significant hurdles when attempting to implement universal guidelines for content moderation related to trafficking. **Data sharing and intelligence coordination require streamlined, multilateral agreements that can bridge both regulatory and enforcement gaps.** Additionally, **privacy laws, such as the GDPR in Europe, present complex challenges** when it comes to monitoring and collecting data on trafficking-related activities. Although designed to protect users' data, these laws can inadvertently protect traffickers by restricting what data can be legally shared between tech companies and law enforcement.

Recruitment of Drivers and Drug Mules through Coded Content

On TikTok, traffickers often craft recruitment content that appeals directly to potential drivers and drug mules by normalising these roles through glamorous or sensationalised portrayals. **Recruitment posts might involve fast-paced videos showcasing the "benefits" of the job, such as luxurious items bought with earnings, images of distant travel locations, or a lifestyle of apparent financial independence.** These visuals provide an illusion of ease and reward, designed to mask the underlying dangers and legal consequences of participating in trafficking operations.

These posts frequently use language that downplays the role's true purpose, presenting it as a simple delivery job without disclosing the illicit nature of the items being transported. To further avoid detection, traffickers use ambiguous phrases like "freelance delivery driver" or "transport role with great travel benefits," appealing to those without prior criminal intent who might be unaware of the implications. By the time recruits realise the full nature of their role, they are often coerced into compliance with threats of violence, exposure, or legal consequences.

Legal and Ethical Implications of Regulation

From a regulatory perspective, the dilemma involves balancing effective monitoring with user privacy rights. **While many argue that tech companies should implement stricter controls, such as compulsory identity verification or enhanced monitoring for suspicious activity, these measures risk alienating legitimate users and creating additional ethical concerns.** Enhanced regulation could help identify trafficking-related activities more efficiently, but it also raises questions about overreach and the potential for abuse.

Efforts to counter trafficking on these platforms require an **adaptive regulatory framework** that can dynamically respond to traffickers' evolving tactics without stifling legitimate online interactions. Solutions could include **greater investment in AI moderation that can identify suspicious patterns, stricter reporting mechanisms for potential victims, and the involvement of third-party watchdogs.** However, for real effectiveness, these approaches need to be globally coordinated, acknowledging that traffickers operate transnationally and adapt quickly to shifts in regulation and enforcement.

In essence, TikTok and similar social platforms have enabled traffickers to scale recruitment efforts globally, reaching thousands of potential victims and accomplices with a single post. This has redefined the digital landscape of trafficking, where law enforcement, tech companies, and governments must cooperate to address both the rapid dissemination of deceptive content and the sophisticated use of these platforms for criminal purposes.

Addressing Technology's Role in Trafficking

The digital age has redefined the parameters of human trafficking, adding layers of complexity to an already intricate crime. From the use of social media for recruitment to the dark web for sales, from encrypted messaging to cryptocurrencies, traffickers have leveraged technology to create a pervasive and resilient network that crosses physical, legal, and moral boundaries. Technology has allowed trafficking to scale globally, enabling a heinous trade that treats human lives as expendable assets.

As we consider solutions to this digital dimension of trafficking, we must recognise that technology itself is not inherently harmful; it is how traffickers exploit it that amplifies their reach and evades detection. Addressing this issue will require innovative regulatory frameworks, advanced technological tools for law enforcement, and an international commitment to disrupting the digital infrastructure that traffickers rely upon.

In the following chapter, I will continue to dissect the influence of globalisation on trafficking, focusing on the ease of cross-border movement and the shifting political landscapes that traffickers exploit. But as this chapter has shown, it is within the digital realm that traffickers have found their most formidable ally.

Chapter 7: The Western Demand: Sex, Labour, and Exploitation

In any discourse on human trafficking, the immediate focus is often, and understandably, on the traffickers themselves those who conduct the deceit, manipulation, and exploitation of vulnerable individuals. They are the visible perpetrators in the shadowy world of trafficking, operating with flagrant disregard for human dignity. However, there is another side to this issue, an uncomfortable and often overlooked truth: for every trafficker who manipulates and exploits, there is a corresponding demand that drives this trade a demand deeply embedded within the Western world's appetite for cheap labour, sexual services, and domestic help.

Western societies, for all their self-professed advancements in human rights and social justice, frequently turn a blind eye to the fact that their own consumer habits, industry practices, and insistence on low-cost services are what sustain this dark economy. This "demand" is not an abstract concept but a tangible force, one that is interwoven with Western daily life in the products they buy, the services they use, and the hidden layers of exploitation upon which their convenience often depends.

Moreover, policies promoting open borders and relaxed immigration oversight have not only failed to curb trafficking but, in many cases, have exacerbated it. A liberal immigration policy, while often enacted with humanitarian intentions, has inadvertently created avenues that traffickers exploit. The promise of opportunity in the West, combined with the lack of stringent border checks or adequate employment verification measures, has created a veritable pipeline for trafficked individuals. These people arrive seeking a new beginning, only to be ensnared in a web of exploitation that serves the economic interests of businesses, industries, and even individual households seeking inexpensive labour.

In this chapter, I intend to confront this uncomfortable reality head-on, exploring how Western demand directly perpetuates exploitation across several major sectors namely, the sex trade, agriculture, construction, and domestic service. I aim to bring to light the complicity of Western society in sustaining this crisis, arguing that for trafficking to truly be addressed, there must be a willingness to examine how Western lifestyles are inextricably linked to the suffering of trafficked individuals.

Labour Costs and the Interests of the Elite

It is essential to address an underlying, often unspoken factor that further complicates the problem: the interests of economic elites who benefit from low-cost, exploitable labour. In a globalised economy that prioritises profit margins and cost-cutting, the financial incentives for large corporations, agribusinesses, and construction firms to use trafficked labour are undeniable. Low labour costs translate to maximised profits, creating a strong, if often covert, alignment between the interests of traffickers and those of Western corporations that rely on cheap labour sources.

For Western elites, cheap labour is a pathway to higher profitability, and trafficked individuals particularly those without legal status or the means to assert their rights represent a controllable and compliant workforce. Many trafficked individuals are unlikely to report abuse for fear of deportation or reprisals from their traffickers, creating a near-ideal labour pool for unscrupulous employers. This dynamic extends well beyond individual businesses; it is a structural issue deeply rooted in Western economic models. Industries that hinge on low-cost, high-output operations are, in some cases, quietly reliant on trafficked labour. From small farms to large-scale construction projects, the elites who benefit from these practices are not incentivised to look too closely at the sources of their labour.

Furthermore, Western economies have been built upon the premise that labour costs should remain low for competitive reasons. The relentless pressure to reduce production costs has led to a permissive attitude towards indirect exploitation, with some industries turning a blind eye to trafficking within their supply chains. This dynamic enables traffickers to thrive within Western economies, assured that the demand for cheap labour is consistent and the risk of backlash from consumers or regulators is relatively low.

The Role of Open Borders in Sustaining Demand

Open borders and relaxed immigration enforcement have added further complexity to the issue of human trafficking. While open border policies may be driven by humanitarian concerns or an idealistic vision of globalisation, they have also created environments in which traffickers can more easily move their victims across borders without significant risk of detection. Western nations with porous or inadequately regulated borders unwittingly facilitate the very systems of exploitation they seek to eradicate.

The allure of opportunity in the West, often magnified by traffickers' false promises, draws individuals from impoverished and conflict-ridden regions. However, without robust border security or enforcement measures, these individuals are more easily ensnared in trafficking networks upon arrival. Once within the borders of a Western nation, they may find themselves effectively invisible, lacking the documentation, language skills, or social connections that could enable them to seek help. In essence, open borders have created an environment in which trafficked individuals are easily exploited in underground economies that cater to the Western appetite for cheap goods and services.

Western societies must confront the reality that their policies, whether intentionally or not, have contributed to the trafficking crisis by creating an environment conducive to exploitation. Furthermore, it is not merely the traffickers or even the companies who benefit from trafficked labour; it is also Western consumers who benefit from the lower prices that result from exploited labour. This reality underscores the importance of viewing human trafficking not only as a criminal issue but as a societal one, in which the demand for low-cost services is as culpable as the supply of vulnerable, exploitable labour.

Confronting the Western Complicity in Trafficking

For Western society to address trafficking meaningfully, it must first grapple with the uncomfortable truth that its demand for low-cost labour, inexpensive goods, and accessible services has fuelled the trafficking crisis. As long as there is a demand for cheap, unregulated labour, traffickers will have ample motivation to supply it. Western nations are complicit in the exploitation of trafficked individuals, whether knowingly or not, through both consumer choices and policy decisions that fail to safeguard vulnerable individuals within their borders.

This chapter seeks to highlight that, while enforcement against traffickers remains essential, it is only part of the solution. Without addressing the Western demand that incentivises trafficking, efforts to end human trafficking will likely remain ineffective. A more profound shift is necessary a shift that recognises the exploitative underpinnings of consumer habits, the willingness of corporations to accept low-cost labour without sufficient scrutiny, and the unintended consequences of open borders. In the chapters that follow, I will examine the potential measures that could curb this demand and explore how Western societies might disentangle themselves from the systems of exploitation they have come to rely upon.

Demand-Driven Exploitation: The Hidden Crisis

While Chapters 1 through 3 provided a foundational understanding of the structure, logistics, and human impact of trafficking, this chapter will confront a rarely acknowledged, yet central, aspect of the problem: the role of Western demand in sustaining the exploitation of trafficked individuals. It is easy to cast traffickers as the sole villains of this dark trade, yet a closer look reveals that trafficking networks are but one cog in a much larger machine. Trafficking is fuelled not merely by opportunistic traffickers but by an enduring, often invisible demand within Western societies for cheap, accessible, and compliant labour. This demand permeates various sectors, from agriculture and construction to domestic work and, most notoriously, the sex trade.

In sectors with high labour demands but scarce protections, trafficked individuals are not an unfortunate anomaly but, rather, the predictable outcome of societal choices and business practices that prioritise cost savings over human dignity. The Western economy, diverse and globalised, absorbs trafficked individuals almost seamlessly, taking advantage of their enforced invisibility in labour-intensive roles. For industries dependent on intensive labour, trafficked individuals represent a silent, vulnerable workforce that enables high-output, low-cost operations a dynamic largely tolerated, if not overtly acknowledged, by both consumers and businesses.

Exploitation as a By-Product of Societal Choices and Business Practices

The consumer habits and business practices prevalent in Western societies create fertile ground for exploitation to thrive. In an economy that demands convenience and affordability, the human cost of labour often takes a back seat. For example, in agriculture, Western consumers expect fresh produce at low prices year-round, regardless of seasonality or the associated labour costs. This expectation drives the agricultural industry to seek out inexpensive, and often unregulated, labour sources to maintain profit margins. Trafficked individuals, frequently undocumented and isolated from legal protections, are ideally positioned to fill this demand. They are easily controlled, expendable, and unlikely to report abuses due to their vulnerable status, making them the workforce of choice in certain labour-intensive sectors.

Construction, too, presents a similar pattern of exploitation. Large-scale infrastructure projects, including commercial and residential developments, demand significant manpower but are cost-sensitive and competitive. In this sector, trafficked individuals are frequently employed for tasks ranging from heavy labour to specialised work, where they are exposed to hazardous conditions and uncompensated overtime without recourse. Companies benefiting from these conditions rarely face scrutiny, as trafficked individuals often remain in the shadows, blending into a transient, unregulated workforce. This "out of sight, out of mind" mentality perpetuates a cycle where exploitation is not merely tolerated but systematically embedded within the very fabric of these industries.

In the realm of domestic services, the demand for affordable, in-home help has led to a troubling prevalence of trafficked individuals in roles such as live-in nannies, cleaners, and caregivers. These individuals are frequently isolated from the outside world, making it exceedingly difficult for them to escape abusive situations. This demand is not confined to any one socio-economic class but spans the spectrum, from middle-class households seeking affordable childcare to wealthy elites expecting around-the-clock domestic help. In many cases, these trafficked individuals are treated as commodities disposable and replaceable while providing indispensable support to the lifestyles of those they serve.

The Sex Trade: Anonymity and Ambiguity as Catalysts of Exploitation

The sex trade stands out as an especially egregious example of how Western demand perpetuates human trafficking. While there is often a perception that sex trafficking is a problem relegated to the shadows, the reality is that Western demand for commercial sexual services creates a lucrative market that traffickers are all too eager to supply. In recent years, the digital age has intensified this demand, with online platforms and apps facilitating the sale and purchase of trafficked individuals with an alarming level of anonymity.

The internet offers a convenient avenue for traffickers to advertise and exploit victims, often under the guise of legitimate escort services. Websites, social media platforms, and classified ads create virtual marketplaces where traffickers can operate with relative impunity. Here, technology serves as a double-edged sword: while it enables traffickers to evade law enforcement, it also allows consumers to purchase trafficked individuals' services without the stigma or risk of public exposure. The inherent anonymity provided by digital platforms further emboldens this demand, creating an ecosystem where trafficked individuals are merely a click away.

Compounding this issue is the ambiguous approach of Western legal systems toward prostitution. Some Western nations have adopted models that decriminalise or even legalise the sale of sexual services, which, while often well-intentioned, can inadvertently create a façade of legitimacy that traffickers exploit. Legal grey areas allow traffickers to hide behind ostensibly legal businesses while continuing to exploit individuals in plain sight. Enforcement efforts, while critical, are often insufficient in addressing the underlying demand that perpetuates this market. As long as consumers continue to seek out these services with little concern for the provenance of the individuals involved, traffickers will find ways to meet that demand, no matter the cost to human dignity.

Addressing Demand: The Unfinished Conversation

While anti-trafficking efforts have traditionally focused on breaking up trafficking networks, apprehending traffickers, and rescuing victims, the foundational issue of demand has largely remained unaddressed. This reluctance to confront demand reflects a wider societal denial and a reluctance to examine the everyday choices, conveniences, and expectations that contribute to the trafficking crisis. Western society's desire for affordable goods, services, and experiences has been prioritised over the ethical and human considerations that should underpin a modern, rights-conscious society.

This chapter aims to provoke a fundamental shift in the way trafficking is understood in the West. By recognising that trafficked individuals are not merely casualties of distant, malevolent actors but are embedded within the Western economy, the conversation around trafficking can shift toward meaningful reform. This will require consumers to confront the consequences of their preferences, for businesses to acknowledge and address the human rights abuses embedded in their supply chains, and for policymakers to implement measures that target not only the traffickers but also the underlying demand driving exploitation.

In the chapters that follow, I will continue to explore the systemic changes required to combat human trafficking effectively. This includes looking at potential regulatory frameworks for industries prone to exploitation, the role of technology in both fuelling and combating trafficking, and, ultimately, the societal attitudes that must shift if trafficking is ever to be eradicated. Until the West is willing to address the uncomfortable truth that its demand perpetuates this crisis, human trafficking will continue to be an embedded, if often invisible, part of the modern economy.

The Sex Trade: How Demand Fuels Exploitation

The sex industry, with its pervasive demand for trafficked individuals, represents perhaps the most visible and controversial intersection of human trafficking and Western consumer appetite. Western societies have long struggled with how to address sex work, employing various approaches from outright criminalisation to models of decriminalisation or regulation. These differing legal responses reflect not only cultural attitudes towards sex work but also a complex moral landscape in which trafficked individuals men, women, and children are caught. Regardless of the approach, the reality remains that traffickers continue to exploit the demand for illicit, affordable, and often anonymous sexual services, using trafficked individuals as pawns in a vast, underground economy that flourishes despite legislative intent.

These trafficked individuals are deceived with false promises, typically of legitimate employment or, in some cases, the guise of a romantic relationship. Once drawn into these webs of deceit, they find themselves ensnared in cycles of exploitation that are difficult to escape. In brothels, massage parlours, and private residences across Western cities, trafficked individuals serve an industry driven by demand that is indifferent to their suffering. This demand sustains a cruel network of brokers, recruiters, and traffickers who see individuals not as human beings but as assets to be exploited until they are no longer profitable.

The Role of Technology in Facilitating Exploitation

As discussed in Chapter 6, the digital age has fundamentally transformed the trafficking landscape, and nowhere is this more apparent than in the sex industry. Technology has given traffickers unprecedented access to platforms where they can advertise services, recruit vulnerable individuals, and communicate securely. Gone are the days when physical locations were the primary sites of exploitation; today, traffickers exploit the anonymity and reach of the internet to conduct business beyond the reach of traditional law enforcement. Platforms that were initially designed for legitimate interactions, including social media sites, messaging apps, and classified ad platforms, are frequently repurposed to facilitate exploitation, with traffickers advertising trafficked individuals to a consumer base that is only a click away.

The use of encrypted messaging apps allows traffickers to communicate with potential clients while concealing their identities, making it incredibly challenging for authorities to trace transactions or identify victims. Meanwhile, the dark web serves as a clandestine marketplace where trafficked individuals are advertised, negotiated over, and sold with the level of anonymity that digital spaces provide. This technological shift has also emboldened consumers, allowing them to seek out illicit services with a sense of impunity, confident that their actions will remain hidden behind layers of encryption and digital anonymity.

Legal Grey Areas and the Commodification of Trafficked Individuals

In many Western nations, the legal landscape surrounding sex work is murky at best. Some countries have adopted regulatory models that allow for legal sex work within certain parameters, while others have criminalised it entirely. Yet, even in regions where sex work is regulated, traffickers are adept at exploiting the legal ambiguities to continue their operations unchecked. The line between consensual sex work and coerced exploitation is easily blurred, and traffickers have become skilled at masking forced prostitution as voluntary work, especially when victims are hesitant to report due to fear of law enforcement, deportation, or reprisal.

Studies have shown that in jurisdictions where prostitution is legally tolerated or overlooked, human trafficking rates are notably higher. The mere existence of a legal sex trade provides traffickers with cover to exploit trafficked individuals, capitalising on the fact that law enforcement is often unwilling or unable to differentiate between voluntary and coerced sex work. Victims are hidden in plain sight, their exploitation disguised as consensual employment a deception that renders them invisible in the eyes of authorities. In these environments, trafficked individuals become mere commodities, a disposable workforce easily replenished as demand dictates.

The commodification of trafficked individuals in the sex trade represents a profound failure of the Western legal and moral framework. The value of these individuals is reduced to their utility within a system that prizes profit over personhood. For traffickers, the calculus is simple: as long as there is a willing consumer base, there will be trafficked individuals to meet that demand. For consumers, the ease with which they can obtain these services creates an illusion that there is nothing wrong, nothing harmful, about their actions. The digital façade of anonymity and the widespread availability of online services combine to make the exploitation of trafficked individuals almost seamless. Demand, in this case, is more than a catalyst; it is the engine that drives the entire system.

The Link Between Demand and Trafficking Rates

The Western appetite for sexual services, coupled with technological advancements, has created an environment where trafficking thrives. Demand studies consistently reveal that where sex work is legally tolerated or inadequately monitored, trafficking rises to meet this demand. Traffickers are well aware of the economic opportunity present in Western countries, where consumers are willing to pay for anonymity and where legal systems may hesitate to confront the complexities of trafficking in the context of sex work.

For instance, countries that have adopted the "Nordic model," criminalising the purchase of sexual services while decriminalising the sale, have seen mixed results in reducing trafficking. While this approach aims to curb demand by punishing the consumer, its effectiveness is often undermined by the very nature of the digital age. The availability of anonymous online platforms enables consumers to continue seeking out trafficked individuals, circumventing legal repercussions with relative ease. In regions where demand remains high and regulatory oversight is limited, trafficked individuals are inevitably drawn to fill the market void. Western consumers, knowingly or unknowingly, are complicit in this dynamic, fuelling an industry that operates beyond the boundaries of legality and morality.

Confronting the Demand: Toward a Societal Shift

Addressing trafficking in the sex industry requires a fundamental shift in Western societal attitudes towards demand. Merely targeting traffickers and attempting to rescue victims addresses only the symptoms of a much larger issue. Until the West acknowledges that its appetite for inexpensive, anonymous, and illicit services perpetuates trafficking, the cycle will continue. There must be a broader awareness among consumers that the services they seek may come at the cost of someone else's freedom and dignity. Educational campaigns, public awareness initiatives, and legislative changes that address consumer behaviour are essential to dismantling the market for trafficked individuals.

Additionally, governments and technology companies must recognise their role in enabling the exploitation of trafficked individuals. Tech companies, in particular, bear a responsibility to monitor and regulate the use of their platforms for trafficking purposes. Enhanced regulations, better reporting mechanisms, and collaboration with law enforcement agencies could serve as powerful deterrents to traffickers using these platforms. However, technology alone cannot curb demand; it must be accompanied by a cultural shift that views trafficked individuals not as commodities, but as victims of a system that fails to protect them.

In this chapter, I have examined the uncomfortable truth that Western demand for sexual services is a driving force behind the trafficking of individuals into the sex industry. The exploitation of trafficked individuals in brothels, massage parlours, and private homes across Western cities is not incidental it is the predictable result of a market where demand far outpaces ethical consideration. As we continue to explore potential solutions in subsequent chapters, it is imperative to recognise that addressing demand is not just an option but a necessity if we hope to dismantle the trafficking networks that feed off Western consumer appetites.

Agriculture: The Demand for Cheap Labour and Its Consequences

Human trafficking in agriculture is a silent yet pervasive issue across the Western world, deeply embedded in the production systems that supply the fresh produce found in supermarkets and markets. While consumers in Europe and North America are generally conscious of food safety and sourcing, few stop to consider the human cost behind the products they buy. The reality is that the relentless drive for low prices in the agricultural industry fuels a demand for cheap, expendable labour a demand that traffickers and exploitative employers readily meet with a workforce often trafficked from impoverished regions around the globe.

As discussed in Chapter 2, human trafficking routes into Western agriculture span continents, bringing individuals from Eastern Europe,

Africa, Asia, and Latin America to work on farms in the United States, Canada, and Western Europe. These individuals, many of whom arrive with little more than the promise of a fair wage, find themselves trapped in exploitative conditions that defy their initial expectations. Traffickers or unscrupulous middlemen play a key role in bridging the gap between impoverished communities and Western agribusinesses, leveraging vulnerabilities whether economic hardship or lack of legal status to create a low-cost labour pool that is highly profitable and easily replaceable.

The Consumer's Blind Spot: Low Prices and Invisible Exploitation

Western consumers, in their demand for inexpensive produce, are largely unaware that the low costs they enjoy are often subsidised by the exploitation of trafficked individuals. The consumer's focus on affordability, exacerbated by the pressures of global competition, forces agricultural enterprises to cut costs wherever possible, with labour being one of the most flexible and vulnerable aspects of the production chain. For the consumer, it is easy to disconnect the low price of a bag of oranges or a punnet of strawberries from the harsh reality that such savings are often made possible through trafficked labour.

Large agricultural corporations, farms, and even smaller-scale producers rely on trafficked labourers as a cost-effective solution to meet the seasonal demand for intensive work that is often shunned by local workers due to its low wages and gruelling conditions. Without legal protections or secure employment rights, trafficked labourers are left at the mercy of their employers. Forced to work in demanding environments, they endure long hours under the sun, inadequate breaks, and substandard living conditions, typically in rural areas that are isolated and difficult to monitor. The lack of visibility both physically and within media narratives allows this issue to persist largely unnoticed by the general public, whose buying habits unknowingly perpetuate the demand for such labour.

The Role of Middlemen and Traffickers in Agricultural Exploitation

In agricultural trafficking, traffickers or middlemen often function as gatekeepers, exerting control over trafficked individuals and insulating the agricultural industry from direct culpability. Acting as the intermediaries, these traffickers typically collect a fee or percentage from trafficked individuals under the guise of "employment services," deceptively positioning themselves as the labourer's primary employer. This arrangement allows agricultural companies to maintain plausible deniability regarding their workforce, effectively shielding themselves from legal consequences and public scrutiny.

The traffickers themselves exert considerable control over these individuals, often confiscating passports, withholding wages, and threatening deportation should they attempt to complain or seek legal redress. Such practices ensure that trafficked workers remain in a state of dependency and fear, unlikely to report their situation to authorities. This arrangement of intimidation and isolation ensures a consistent supply of cheap labour to meet agricultural demand while rendering these workers invisible, not only to enforcement agencies but also to a broader public unaware of the exploitation underpinning their groceries.

Minimal Protections and Limited Recourse for Trafficked Agricultural Workers

Agricultural workers who are trafficked into Western economies frequently find themselves devoid of legal protections, exploited by an agricultural industry that operates with minimal oversight. Many trafficked workers are undocumented, having entered the country illegally or on temporary visas that tie them to a specific employer, leaving them highly vulnerable to exploitation. Without legal status, trafficked workers face immense barriers to seeking assistance or asserting their rights; for them, any attempt to escape could lead to deportation or imprisonment, rather than protection.

Living conditions for trafficked agricultural workers are often deplorable. Workers may be housed in overcrowded or unsanitary facilities, with inadequate access to necessities. Some employers even charge rent for these accommodations, deducting it from already. meagre wages and ensuring that trafficked individuals are perpetually in debt. Reports reveal that wage withholding is commonplace, with employers or traffickers refusing to pay workers for weeks or months to maintain control over them. The threat of deportation, combined with an absence of accessible legal channels, renders trafficked individuals effectively voiceless within a system designed to overlook their plight.

Consumer Culpability: The Hidden Cost of Low-Cost Produce

The demand for trafficked labour within the agricultural industry raises significant ethical concerns about the responsibility of consumers in perpetuating this cycle of exploitation. Consumers in Western nations may find it difficult to connect their daily purchases to human trafficking, yet every low-cost transaction unwittingly sustains an agricultural system that thrives on the availability of vulnerable, low-wage workers. Unlike in the sex industry, where direct engagement with trafficked individuals is often visible and debated, the exploitation within agriculture is obscured by distance, as consumers encounter only the polished end product on grocery store shelves.

Each purchase made without consideration of labour practices and sourcing perpetuates a market structure that benefits from trafficked labour. Corporations and consumers alike contribute to an economy where trafficked workers are treated as expendable, serving as a hidden subsidy for the West's preference for low-cost goods. As such, there is a disconnect between the Western public's values largely opposed to human trafficking and their actions in the marketplace, where price typically takes precedence over ethical considerations. The minimal public awareness around this issue shields it from being challenged or reformed, allowing the exploitation to continue unimpeded.

Towards Greater Accountability: Addressing Demand in Agricultural Trafficking

To reduce demand for trafficked labour within agriculture, the onus cannot solely fall upon traffickers and employers; consumers and regulatory bodies must also bear responsibility. Consumers, particularly in Western societies, wield significant influence in shaping market trends. Public pressure, ethical awareness campaigns, and stricter scrutiny of agricultural sourcing can help reduce the industry's reliance on trafficked individuals. For consumers, this might mean paying slightly higher prices or supporting brands that uphold fair labour practices. It also requires a shift in mindset, recognising that cost-cutting measures in one part of the world often result in human suffering elsewhere.

Governments, too, must prioritise the protection of vulnerable workers and ensure that industries heavily reliant on trafficked labour are held accountable. Labour laws and regulatory oversight need to be reinforced to address the specific vulnerabilities of trafficked individuals within the agricultural sector, providing them with avenues for legal recourse, housing protections, and wage guarantees. Stringent monitoring and penalties for farms and companies that engage in trafficked labour could serve as a deterrent to exploitative practices, pushing companies toward more ethical business models.

In sum, Western consumers, corporations, and governments must confront the uncomfortable reality that demand for cheap produce often supports a system of exploitation. The fresh fruits and vegetables on our tables come at a cost far beyond what is reflected on the price tag one that is paid by trafficked individuals forced to work under oppressive conditions, often out of sight and out of mind. Addressing agricultural trafficking requires more than penalising traffickers; it demands a fundamental shift in how the West approaches food production and consumption, with greater accountability for the true human cost behind the goods we so often take for granted.

Construction: The Infrastructure of Exploitation

Construction, a sector foundational to the rapid urban development characteristic of Western economies, relies heavily on trafficked labour to meet its ever-growing demands for affordability and flexibility. The market's emphasis on cost efficiency and speed has created an environment where trafficked individuals often foreign workers from impoverished regions are drawn into exploitative roles. This hidden workforce fuels countless projects across the USA, Europe, and the UK, often working on high-profile developments under conditions that sharply contradict labour laws and human rights standards.

The need for trafficked labour in construction is linked to two primary drivers. First, Western countries are in constant need of infrastructure upgrades, housing developments, and urban expansion to keep pace with growing populations and evolving economies. Second, the competition among contractors to secure projects with the most economical bids has pressured companies to find ways to minimise labour costs, making trafficked workers a seemingly "efficient" resource. While laws in these countries mandate fair treatment and protective measures for all workers, trafficked individuals are frequently excluded from these safeguards by the covert nature of their employment and their often precarious legal status.

The Role of Traffickers and Unethical Contractors in Construction Exploitation

Traffickers serve as a key link between vulnerable populations and Western construction companies, providing a cheap, compliant workforce that is unlikely to resist exploitation due to a lack of legal protections and language barriers. Many trafficked individuals enter the construction industry under false promises lured by the prospect of stable income, accommodation, and fair working conditions. Upon arrival, however, they find themselves bound to exploitative employers, with passports confiscated and wages withheld as a means of control. Contractors may employ these trafficked individuals directly, but more commonly, they outsource the hiring to third-party labour agencies that specialise in recruiting foreign workers, allowing companies to sidestep direct responsibility for the welfare of these individuals.

These middlemen, often with connections to organised crime or other illegal networks, enforce strict control over trafficked individuals, who live and work under near-constant surveillance. Many workers are forced into debt bondage, with fees for transportation, documentation, and accommodation deducted from their already low wages, ensuring they remain trapped in a cycle of dependency. The threat of deportation or violence hangs over them, keeping trafficked workers compliant and fearful, thereby allowing traffickers and unscrupulous contractors to profit from their forced labour without facing significant resistance.

Gruelling Conditions and a Culture of Silence

The conditions faced by trafficked workers in construction are harsh and unregulated, with many subjected to long hours of physically demanding labour in dangerous environments. While local workers are typically covered by safety regulations and protected by trade unions, trafficked workers are systematically excluded from these protections, and forced to operate in hazardous conditions with limited access to safety equipment or training. Injuries are common, but few trafficked workers seek medical assistance due to fear of exposure and deportation.

Living conditions for these individuals are often deplorable, with cramped, unsanitary accommodations provided by their employers or traffickers. In many cases, these workers are housed in remote locations near construction sites, isolated from local communities and devoid of support networks. This isolation serves the dual purpose of controlling the workers while shielding their existence from public scrutiny. Such exploitation is facilitated by a widespread culture of silence in the industry, where even legitimate companies may turn a blind eye to labour violations to keep projects on schedule and within budget.

Regulatory Gaps and the Complexity of Enforcement

While Western nations have established robust frameworks to protect workers' rights, the enforcement of these laws in the construction industry is often hindered by the opacity of trafficking networks and the indirect hiring practices that obscure accountability. Labour inspections, where they occur, are rarely equipped to detect the nuanced forms of coercion and control exercised over trafficked individuals, especially when these workers are employed by subcontractors or temporary agencies. This fragmented employment structure complicates legal enforcement and enables unethical contractors to exploit trafficked workers with minimal risk of legal repercussions.

Furthermore, the prevalence of trafficked labour in construction is often underreported due to the vested interests of both employers and traffickers in maintaining the status quo. Contractors operating under tight deadlines and constrained budgets may actively avoid scrutiny, knowing that their success often hinges on minimising labour costs.

The ability to complete projects on time and under budget is highly valued, sometimes eclipsing concerns for worker welfare, especially in a competitive industry where financial incentives often take precedence over ethical considerations.

Consumer and Corporate Responsibility in Curbing Construction Exploitation

The demand for trafficked labour in construction not only reflects a failure of enforcement but also points to a deeper issue within Western society: the prioritisation of economic efficiency over human rights. Western consumers, unknowingly complicit in the exploitation of trafficked labour, rarely consider the human cost of the homes, offices, and infrastructure they inhabit. While the consumer's connection to trafficking in construction is less direct than in industries like agriculture or the sex trade, there remains an implicit responsibility to question and influence the ethics of construction companies and their labour practices.

Corporations, particularly those managing large development projects, have an ethical duty to ensure that their supply chains and hiring practices do not perpetuate human trafficking. Transparent hiring practices, regular audits, and strict vetting of subcontractors can serve as crucial steps in mitigating the exploitation of trafficked workers. Increasingly, investors and stakeholders in the construction sector are recognising the importance of ethical standards and labour compliance as essential to sustainable business practices. Informed consumers and industry oversight can apply pressure on companies to uphold higher ethical standards and deter traffickers and unethical contractors from exploiting vulnerable individuals.

The Broader Implications of Trafficking in Construction

Human trafficking in the construction industry has far-reaching implications that go beyond the immediate suffering of exploited individuals. The widespread use of trafficked labour undermines the wages and working conditions of legal, local workers, creating a race to the bottom in labour standards and reducing job security for all. It erodes public confidence in labour laws and regulatory systems, fostering an environment where the exploitation of vulnerable individuals is tolerated or ignored. Furthermore, the presence of trafficked labour distorts the market, allowing companies that rely on exploitation to undercut ethical businesses, perpetuating an unethical competitive advantage.

To counter these implications, there must be a concerted effort to address the demand that fuels trafficking in construction. This involves not only strict enforcement of labour laws but also a societal shift toward valuing fair treatment and human dignity over marginal financial gains. Governments, corporations, and consumers alike have roles to play in dismantling the exploitative structures that allow human trafficking to persist within the construction industry. Without addressing the demand for trafficked labour, the industry will remain fertile ground for exploitation, rendering the achievements of Western development and urbanisation tainted by the suffering of trafficked individuals hidden behind scaffolds and construction cranes.

Domestic Service: Hidden Labour, Hidden Exploitation

The trafficking of individuals for domestic labour is a particularly insidious facet of Western demand for low-cost, compliant workers, a need often met by the wealthiest households. Unlike more visible sectors, exploitation within private homes remains shielded from public scrutiny, cloaked by the privacy and autonomy associated with one's domain. This demand for domestic help including roles as housekeepers, nannies, caretakers, and cooks has fostered an environment where trafficked individuals, predominantly women from impoverished or conflict-ridden regions, are highly vulnerable to exploitation. The isolation of trafficked workers in this setting not only perpetuates cycles of abuse but also obscures the scale of this hidden crisis.

The Role of the Wealthy in Engaging Trafficked Domestic Workers

Wealthier households often drive the demand for trafficked domestic workers, drawn by the promise of affordable, reliable, and unobtrusive labour that accommodates the lifestyle and expectations of the affluent. In many cases, these trafficked individuals are brought to Western countries under seemingly legitimate channels, such as temporary visas or sponsorship programmes that tie them to a particular household. These arrangements, often requiring the worker to reside on the property, reinforce an employer's control, creating a de facto bond of dependency and isolation that traffickers or unethical employers exploit.

Once inside the private confines of the home, trafficked domestic workers are frequently denied access to external resources or contact with others who might assist them. Wealthy employers who engage in this practice may rationalise low or withheld pay and excessive demands as part of the employee's sponsorship arrangement, exploiting the worker's unfamiliarity with local laws and social networks. This dynamic renders trafficked individuals vulnerable to verbal abuse, threats of deportation, or even physical violence, making it nearly impossible for them to escape or report their exploitation.

The Complex Realities of "Sponsorship" and Dependency

The sponsorship model, often touted as a means of providing work opportunities to those from underprivileged backgrounds, has in practice become a tool for control in many instances. These sponsorships bind the worker's legal status to a single employer, who can then leverage this dependence to exert almost complete control over the individual. Workers may arrive believing they are embarking on a new opportunity, only to find themselves in exploitative situations with few alternatives. For trafficked domestic workers, the threat of losing both their jobs and legal status serves as a powerful deterrent against seeking help or reporting abuse. Often, passports are confiscated upon arrival, a practice designed to prevent workers from fleeing and further cementing their dependency.

In many cases, trafficked domestic workers are coerced into gruelling schedules with little regard for personal well-being. They may work upwards of 16 hours per day, handling multiple roles cleaning, cooking, child care, and elder care without respite. For wealthy employers, the high degree of control over domestic workers can create a sense of entitlement, emboldening them to dismiss complaints, ignore basic human rights, or view trafficked workers as a mere "resource" that can be easily replaced. This dynamic reinforces a cycle in which trafficked workers, isolated within the home, experience extreme forms of exploitation that would be harder to conceal in more public settings.

Exploitation and Abuse in the Privacy of the Home

The abuse that trafficked domestic workers endure is compounded by their isolation. Unlike workers in factories or agricultural settings, domestic labourers are rarely seen by the public or their communities. This lack of visibility enables wealthy employers to enforce harsh working conditions without fear of exposure or consequence. Domestic workers who suffer abuse or exploitation have limited options to seek help, particularly when they are confined within gated properties or restricted from leaving without the employer's permission.

Because their workplace is also their residence, trafficked domestic workers face an unrelenting cycle of servitude, often with no designated working hours and minimal personal privacy. The psychological toll of this constant control is severe, and traffickers and unethical employers exploit the mental and physical exhaustion of workers to maintain control. Additionally, in some cases, trafficked individuals endure verbal and emotional abuse designed to undermine their sense of worth and independence, leaving them increasingly reliant on their exploiters for survival.

The Failure of Labour Laws and Regulatory Oversight

While many Western countries have enacted labour protections, these are notoriously difficult to enforce within the domestic sphere. Labour laws often exempt households from oversight, and inspections, where they do exist, may be limited to industries rather than individual homes. This lack of regulation means that trafficked domestic workers, who are already isolated from external resources, are left without the protective mechanisms afforded to other sectors. Even when incidents of abuse or exploitation are reported, it can be challenging to secure the evidence needed to hold employers accountable.

Regulatory gaps further exacerbate the problem, as the legal framework for addressing human trafficking in domestic labour settings is often fragmented or insufficiently resourced. In some cases, trafficked workers are repatriated without a full investigation, particularly if their legal status has lapsed, inadvertently protecting the employer from prosecution and perpetuating the cycle of trafficking. Wealthy employers, meanwhile, often possess the resources to shield themselves from scrutiny, whether through legal representation, social influence, or simply the privacy of their own homes.

The Broader Implications of Trafficking in Domestic Labour

The trafficking of domestic workers not only represents a human rights crisis but also highlights the disparities in wealth and power that underpin Western societies. In a socio-economic landscape where the wealthy can evade accountability for exploiting trafficked individuals, there exists a moral and ethical failure that extends beyond the household. The ability to control and exploit individuals within the intimate space of the home reveals a disturbing undercurrent of inequality, where the financial and social status of wealthy employers shields them from the laws designed to protect vulnerable populations.

The issue also raises important questions about consumer awareness and accountability. While the general public may be vocal about human trafficking in more visible industries, such as agriculture or construction, the exploitation of domestic workers remains largely unaddressed. The societal deference to wealth and privacy has allowed trafficking within households to persist with minimal public condemnation, perpetuating the notion that trafficked domestic workers are an invisible, acceptable "cost" of luxury.

Addressing the Demand for Trafficked Domestic Labour

Addressing the demand for trafficked domestic workers in Western households requires a multifaceted approach that includes stronger regulatory oversight, legal reform, and societal awareness. Governments must establish clearer legal frameworks to protect domestic workers, closing the loopholes that allow trafficked individuals to be exploited in private settings. Regular inspections and reporting channels specific to domestic labour could help alleviate the risks associated with isolated working conditions.

Raising public awareness about the plight of trafficked domestic workers, particularly among the affluent communities that are most likely to employ them, is also essential. Consumer responsibility extends into the home, where the engagement of trafficked workers for domestic tasks should be recognised as an unacceptable practice, regardless of its invisibility. Greater accountability and transparency from hiring agencies, combined with harsher penalties for employers who exploit trafficked individuals, are crucial steps in dismantling this deeply entrenched form of exploitation.

In conclusion, the trafficking of domestic workers within private households highlights a troubling intersection of wealth, power, and human rights abuses that Western society has yet to fully confront. The affluence of the wealthy has fostered a demand for cheap, compliant labour that traffickers are all too willing to supply. By recognising and addressing how private households contribute to trafficking, Western nations can take a vital step towards dismantling this hidden industry of human exploitation.

Turning a Blind Eye: The Supply Chains of Exploitation

Human trafficking's tentacles stretch far beyond the visible instances of direct exploitation; they permeate the supply chains of countless consumer products sold across Western markets. In an age of mass consumption, Western companies, especially those in fashion, technology, agriculture, and manufacturing, rely heavily on intricate global supply chains to maintain competitive pricing. While corporate responsibility standards are often touted as safeguards against exploitation, they have consistently fallen short, allowing trafficked labour and severe exploitation to persist in production hubs throughout Asia, Africa, and Latin America.

A further concern arises when examining the involvement of multinational corporations and their political influence on mass migration policies. Some companies appear to support and fund progressive political parties, parties that advocate for more open or lax migration policies, ostensibly as a means of supporting humanitarian goals or advancing diversity. However, the influx of undocumented labour effectively offers a continuous supply of cheap, exploitable workers for industries that benefit from flexible, low-cost labour. Such practices raise ethical questions about corporate donations to political causes, as these align with business interests that benefit from a more permissive approach to illegal migration.

The Reality of Trafficked Labour Embedded in Supply Chains

Western consumers are largely unaware of the human cost behind the inexpensive goods they purchase. In the garment industry, for example, "fast fashion" brands have production chains spread across developing countries where trafficked individuals may be forced into gruelling, unsafe work for little to no pay. Labour abuses in these regions range from debt bondage to outright slavery, where traffickers coerce individuals through deception or violence. Such practices are sustained by Western demand for affordable, quickly-produced clothing, electronics, and even food products.

Electronics production also relies on vast supply chains, with companies sourcing components from multiple locations. Many of these components are manufactured or assembled in exploitative conditions by trafficked workers or impoverished labourers, often under threat or coercion. This is especially evident in the mining industry, where trafficked labourers in countries across Africa are made to extract rare minerals used in electronic devices, from smartphones to laptops. The Western market's insatiable appetite for affordable, high-tech products drives demand, leading corporations to prioritise low-cost production over ethical labour practices.

The Influence of Corporate Interests on Migration Policies

Beyond indirect involvement in trafficking via supply chains, Western corporations also appear to play an active role in shaping policies that facilitate a steady flow of exploitable labour. Some of the world's largest corporations make significant political donations, predominantly to parties and candidates who favour more lenient immigration policies. These companies then benefit from an increase in undocumented workers who, due to their precarious legal status, may be forced to work under exploitative conditions without the protection of labour laws.

For example, industries such as agriculture, construction, hospitality, and domestic services have come to rely heavily on undocumented migrant labour to fill positions that are generally lower-paying and labour-intensive. Political support for mass migration, under the guise of humanitarian aid or economic enrichment, effectively fuels this demand for illegal, underpaid, and vulnerable workers. This creates a cycle wherein political donations from companies benefiting from cheap labour support policies that perpetuate the arrival of an exploitable workforce.

Corporate Double Standards: Public Declarations vs. Private Actions

While multinational corporations may publicly denounce human trafficking and tout corporate social responsibility, their actions often reveal a starkly different reality. Many Western companies have supply chains that are incredibly difficult to monitor, particularly in developing regions where regulatory oversight is weak or non-existent. Some companies may engage in surface-level audits or compliance checks to satisfy public relations requirements, but enforcement remains lax, and actual conditions often remain unchanged.

Reports of exploitation are frequent in industries known for their outsourced supply chains, including textiles, electronics, and food production. In many cases, traffickers operate within complex subcontracting networks, making it easy for Western corporations to disclaim direct responsibility while still reaping the benefits of lower production costs. The resulting complicity between traffickers, unscrupulous suppliers, and corporate interests ensures that trafficked labour remains an "unseen" yet integral component of supply chains, creating low-cost goods for Western markets.

The Cost of Demand: How Western Consumption Fuels Exploitation

At the heart of this problem is Western consumer demand for affordable goods, which effectively sustains trafficking networks around the world. The vast disparity between the low costs of production and the high standards of living in Western societies has established a global economic structure where trafficked labour becomes a viable solution to bridge that gap. The allure of cheaper products drives companies to maintain supply chains that cut costs at every level, even if this means turning a blind eye to the trafficking embedded within those chains.

This system is especially pronounced in competitive markets where profit margins are tight and global competition fierce. To remain competitive, many corporations opt to source products from regions where labour is undervalued or unregulated, knowing that trafficked individuals can be used to fill high-demand, low-wage positions. Western consumers, for their part, play an indirect but crucial role by purchasing these goods, often unaware that their "bargains" come at the expense of exploited individuals.

Solutions and the Path Forward

While some progress has been made to address trafficking within supply chains, these efforts are often hindered by the vast, opaque networks spanning multiple countries and jurisdictions. Transparency initiatives, such as ethical sourcing certifications, are a step forward but often fall short of covering entire supply chains. Western governments could strengthen anti-trafficking legislation that holds corporations accountable for all tiers of their supply chains, not just the immediate suppliers.

In addition to government action, corporations themselves bear a moral responsibility to enforce more rigorous checks and penalties for violations within their supply chains. True accountability would mean adopting zero-tolerance policies for trafficking at all levels, supported by independent audits that involve local, on-the-ground investigations. Additionally, consumers can play a role by supporting businesses that commit to fair trade and ethical labour practices, even if this means higher prices.

Ultimately, a cultural shift in consumer expectations towards supporting ethical production, combined with stricter enforcement of corporate accountability, could begin to dismantle the deeply embedded trafficking networks within Western supply chains. The true cost of goods should reflect the fair and humane treatment of workers, rather than exploitation masked by corporate and political collusion. Addressing these issues requires coordinated action across governments, corporations, and consumers, to ensure that the pursuit of profit no longer comes at the expense of vulnerable individuals.

The Uncomfortable Truth

Western demand for trafficked individuals cannot be ignored if we are to make meaningful strides against this pervasive crime. Each of the sectors explored sex work, agriculture, construction, domestic service, and global supply chains reveals a pattern in which exploitation is not an aberration but an intrinsic aspect of meeting Western needs and wants. Addressing this demand is a crucial step toward a more comprehensive approach to combatting human trafficking. Without confronting the economic forces that make trafficking profitable, the West will remain ensnared in the very systems of exploitation it condemns.

In subsequent chapters, I will explore potential remedies, policy reforms, and cultural shifts that could mitigate this demand. But as this chapter has shown, until the West recognises its role in driving the demand for trafficked individuals, human trafficking will remain an indelible, uncomfortable shadow across our society.

Chapter 8: Human Trafficking and Immigration: The Blurred Lines

In examining human trafficking, we reach a critical intersection with immigration a junction fraught with complexities, challenges, and human vulnerability. As we have seen in earlier chapters, human trafficking is not only a heinous crime but also an intricate network of exploitation, sustained by demand, profit, and sometimes even the very systems meant to counteract it. This chapter explores how the phenomenon of immigration, particularly illegal immigration, often collides with trafficking, creating blurred lines between the two. In some cases, traffickers prey on those who attempt the journey to a safer or more prosperous life. In others, well-meaning immigration policies in the West inadvertently leave migrants more exposed to traffickers' manipulations. We must also consider the difficulties law enforcement and regulatory bodies face in distinguishing between victims of trafficking and illegal immigrants, a challenge that allows traffickers to exploit both groups with startling efficacy.

The Intersection of Trafficking and Immigration

Human trafficking and immigration often intersect in situations where individuals are forced to leave behind unbearable circumstances in search of stability or the possibility of a better life. Migrants fleeing from impoverished or politically unstable regions are particularly vulnerable to exploitation by traffickers. Whether these individuals are driven by conflict, famine, persecution, or simply a lack of economic opportunity, they often find themselves in desperate need of safe passage and survival. In their vulnerability, they are compelled to trust "smugglers" or "agents" who promise not only transit but the hope of employment and security in Western countries. Yet, this reliance on intermediaries in environments where legal protection is non-existent or inadequate often leads to exploitation, manipulation, and, ultimately, trafficking.

This shared foundation of displacement and desperation creates a grey area where trafficking and illegal immigration overlap in ways that make it exceedingly difficult to draw distinctions. For many individuals, especially those unfamiliar with immigration regulations or the dangers that lie ahead, the line between consensual movement and forced exploitation can blur. Victims of trafficking may not even realise the nature of their entrapment until it is far too late; promises of employment or freedom morph into forced labour, sexual exploitation, or domestic servitude under harsh conditions from which escape is nearly impossible.

As we delved into in Chapter 2, traffickers often take advantage of well-established smuggling routes to move people across borders, whether by land, sea, or air. These routes, while perilous, are frequented by undocumented migrants as well as trafficked individuals, allowing traffickers to hide their victims within larger migration flows, often escaping the notice of authorities. This overlap between trafficking victims and undocumented migrants creates logistical and ethical dilemmas for governments attempting to balance border security with the imperative to protect victims of trafficking.

Traffickers, well aware of the risks migrants face, actively exploit these hardships to entrap their victims. The journey itself is perilous, with land routes traversing deserts, dense forests, and border checkpoints where safety is compromised at every turn. Many migrants attempt dangerous sea crossings on overcrowded and unseaworthy vessels, often without adequate food, water, or medical supplies. These vessels, sometimes organised by traffickers themselves, have high mortality rates due to capsizing, dehydration, or exposure to the elements. Air transit, though less common, also poses significant risks; migrants are frequently transported with forged documents, leading to detention, extortion, and, ultimately, ensnarement by traffickers at various transit points.

Western immigration policies, while primarily intended to curtail illegal immigration, can inadvertently exacerbate migrants' vulnerability to trafficking. These policies typically involve rigorous border enforcement, limited legal pathways, and harsh penalties for illegal entry, which leave migrants with few legitimate options for crossing into destination countries. As borders become more fortified and migration pathways more restricted, individuals with pressing needs or minimal resources often feel they have no choice but to engage traffickers who promise safe transit through illegal means. This paradoxical outcome aided by restrictive policies often forces people into even riskier channels, increasing their dependence on smugglers or traffickers who thrive in an environment of fear and isolation.

Traffickers understand the migrant's plight intimately, and they are adept at exploiting every moment of desperation. Migrants who successfully evade detection at borders frequently discover that they are not free in their destination country; rather, they remain beholden to traffickers who exert control through fear, coercion, and financial bondage. This enforced dependence can be particularly severe for those who arrive without documents or the legal status necessary to seek refuge. Fear of deportation keeps victims isolated, ensuring they remain hidden within underground economies and unable to seek assistance. Traffickers further entrench this control by withholding wages, threatening loved ones in their home countries, or using violence, thereby stripping individuals of agency and making escape nearly impossible.

In effect, Western immigration policies, despite their intentions to regulate migration and protect national security, often create an unintended pipeline for trafficking. By driving people into the shadows, these policies create conditions where traffickers can operate with relative impunity, knowing that their victims are trapped not only by physical and financial constraints but also by their lack of options within the legal system. Without safe, transparent migration routes or adequate support structures for migrants who have experienced trauma or exploitation, traffickers continue to operate within these blurred lines, perpetuating cycles of exploitation that are extraordinarily difficult to untangle.

Exploitation of Migrant Populations

Migrants, whether entering a country through legal channels or undocumented pathways, represent one of the most vulnerable demographics worldwide. Their vulnerability is amplified by a complex web of challenges, including a lack of social protections, limited language proficiency, and scarce financial resources. These individuals, in their attempts to gain a foothold in unfamiliar and often unwelcoming environments, frequently end up in marginalised communities where the prospect of stable, fair employment remains elusive. Those who manage to find work are often relegated to precarious, low-paying jobs, and many find themselves without any employment at all. This economic instability, coupled with their limited social support networks, makes migrants especially susceptible to exploitation by traffickers who lure them with promises of security, fair wages, housing, and a new beginning only to trap them in cycles of debt and coercion that prove nearly impossible to escape.

Once under the control of traffickers, these individuals are often forced into jobs that fall well below humane standards of labour, with wages and working conditions that strip them of basic rights and dignity. Traffickers typically enforce compliance through debt bondage, charging exorbitant fees for transport, housing, or supposed "protection." When combined with physical intimidation, threats of deportation, and even violence against them or their families, these tactics ensure that victims remain trapped in exploitative conditions. This exploitation is endemic across various industries, as examined in Chapter 7. Sectors such as agriculture, construction, and domestic work often employ trafficked individuals who are virtually invisible within the workforce, their legal status precarious and their safety and rights ignored. For migrants, this vulnerability is intensified by the fact that reporting abuse could very well lead to deportation rather than assistance, leaving them with no legitimate means of seeking help or justice.

Without access to the legal protections afforded to citizens or documented immigrants, migrants are left at the mercy of traffickers who exploit the implicit protection their victims' invisibility provides. Often unable to speak the local language fluently, with minimal knowledge of their rights or local labour laws, and with limited understanding of support systems, they are left with few resources. This isolation allows traffickers to exert control with a devastating degree of impunity, as migrants remain fearful of attracting attention from law enforcement, which could result in detention or deportation. Western immigration policies, aimed primarily at controlling undocumented immigration, thus inadvertently serve as an enforcement mechanism for traffickers by perpetuating the silence of the exploited and driving trafficking further underground.

Furthermore, the issue is exacerbated by lax criminal enforcement against traffickers. Many Western countries maintain strict immigration policies yet fall short of actively prosecuting traffickers. Despite public awareness campaigns and anti-trafficking laws, traffickers often evade serious legal consequences, leaving their victims without justice or protection. Low conviction rates and minimal enforcement encourage traffickers to continue operating with relative impunity, knowing that the risk of criminal prosecution remains low. This failure in enforcement, combined with stringent immigration policies, creates a double bind for trafficked individuals: they are both too vulnerable to seek help and too at risk of punishment to attempt escape. Without robust legal deterrents, traffickers face little fear of retribution, enabling them to exploit victims who lack the protection of documented status.

Western immigration frameworks, though designed to uphold security, unintentionally become conduits for exploitation when enforcement is misaligned. Instead of addressing the problem at its root by focusing on traffickers and ensuring comprehensive protection for vulnerable populations, current practices often result in the marginalisation of migrants who then become prime targets for exploitation. Traffickers are aware of this gap and exploit it, positioning themselves as the "safe" alternative for migrants who fear legal authorities more than the traffickers themselves. To genuinely address the intertwined issues of trafficking and immigration, policies must be re-evaluated to ensure they do not inadvertently shield traffickers while marginalising the very individuals they intend to protect.

As explored in previous chapters, human trafficking is not a single-issue problem; it is deeply intertwined with economic disparities, social vulnerabilities, and the legislative landscape. In Chapter 5, we discussed how corruption within governance and law enforcement compounds the trafficking problem by allowing traffickers to operate unchecked. This situation is intensified for migrant populations, who remain effectively unprotected from both traffickers and corrupt officials. Without a unified, targeted approach that includes stringent enforcement against traffickers, more comprehensive support for migrants, and systemic protections against corruption, Western immigration policies will continue to unintentionally contribute to the silence and suffering of trafficking victims. A proactive approach is essential one that recognises the economic, social, and legal complexities of trafficking and immigration and works to dismantle traffickers' influence by addressing the root vulnerabilities they exploit.

Western Immigration Policies: Unintended Consequences

Western immigration policies are frequently crafted to prevent illegal entry, safeguard borders, and uphold national security. However, the stringent barriers created to achieve these goals often have unintended consequences, particularly in the realm of human trafficking. By fortifying borders and tightening legal avenues of entry, these policies leave many migrants with limited and often dangerous options, making them more likely to fall prey to traffickers who promise what appears to be a safe passage and a legitimate chance at building a new life. Yet, the reality of these arrangements frequently devolves into coercion and exploitation as traffickers control migrants through threats, debt bondage, or outright physical force.

As discussed in previous chapters, particularly in Chapter 2 on trafficking routes and Chapter 6 on the role of technology, traffickers leverage every means at their disposal to reach and exploit these vulnerable individuals. Closed or highly restricted borders create a lucrative market for traffickers who exploit these barriers by offering "alternatives" that quickly transform into exploitative arrangements. The traffickers' ability to advertise and manage these exploitative services is amplified by modern technology: encrypted messaging applications, social media, and even the dark web facilitate recruitment, coordination, and control over their victims. Traffickers now utilise online networks to create false job advertisements, promising legitimate work and stable income to individuals desperate for an escape from dire conditions at home. Once lured in, these migrants find themselves caught in exploitative work, isolated from support, and often without a clear path to freedom.

Open-border policies, as implemented by recent administrations, particularly the current White House add yet another layer of complexity. While such policies are intended to offer sanctuary and opportunities, they also create conditions that traffickers can exploit. The allure of an accessible border can act as a draw for migrants from around the world who, believing that entry will be straightforward, undertake arduous journeys only to find themselves stranded or worse. Without sufficient infrastructure or processing capabilities to handle large influxes, many migrants are left in limbo, their vulnerable status creating a fertile ground for traffickers to step in. Under the guise of "helping" migrants navigate the system or "connecting" them to work, traffickers take advantage of gaps in border enforcement and processing, exploiting those who arrive with the hope of a safer future.

In addition, the availability of social benefits in Western countries, particularly in the United States and Europe, acts as another pull factor for migrants, and traffickers use this as a part of their manipulative tactics. Traffickers often promise migrants access to housing, healthcare, and social benefits upon arrival, knowing that many are drawn to the stability and security these provisions suggest. However, upon arrival, traffickers often withhold identification documents or other means of accessing these services, keeping victims in a dependent and compromised state. For many migrants, the prospect of safety and stability becomes an unattainable dream as traffickers use social benefits as bait, turning these individuals into sources of profit rather than individuals deserving of the support they were promised.

The cyclical nature of these issues is further exacerbated by the lax enforcement of trafficking laws and low conviction rates against traffickers. Western countries may devote resources to securing borders and detaining undocumented migrants but often fall short when it comes to prosecuting the traffickers themselves. This failure to crack down on traffickers emboldens them, allowing the cycle of exploitation to continue unchecked. Traffickers operate with a degree of impunity, understanding that while migrants may face swift deportation, the legal repercussions for those orchestrating trafficking operations are minimal. This lack of enforcement against traffickers perpetuates a system where migrants, fearful of deportation or prosecution, remain trapped in exploitative conditions, unable to seek help without risking their precarious standing.

Furthermore, heightened immigration enforcement aimed at deporting undocumented individuals unintentionally drives trafficking further underground. Migrants, many of whom are already isolated by language and cultural barriers, are left with limited avenues for reporting abuse, especially when traffickers instil in them a fear of law enforcement. Traffickers continually reinforce this fear, making it clear to their victims that any interaction with authorities will lead to detention or deportation. As a result, migrants are pushed into an almost invisible state of existence where exploitation continues unchecked, shielded by the very immigration policies meant to deter illegal entry. In such an environment, victims, already isolated and vulnerable, feel they have nowhere to turn, and traffickers take full advantage of this silence.

The complexity of these intersecting issues reveals a systemic problem within Western immigration policies. Policies that aim to prevent illegal immigration inadvertently drive migrants into traffickers' hands by creating conditions that push individuals into vulnerable situations. Border restrictions, limited legal pathways, and strict enforcement measures compound the risks for migrants while emboldening traffickers to operate with minimal interference. Addressing this multifaceted issue requires not only a focus on border security but also a comprehensive approach to dismantling traffickers' influence by aligning enforcement efforts with support for victims. To create lasting change, Western policies must prioritise both the prosecution of traffickers and the protection of those they exploit.

The Blurring of Legal Definitions: Victims or Illegal Immigrants?

Identifying trafficking victims within illegal immigrant populations poses profound legal and ethical challenges for law enforcement and immigration officials. Human trafficking, characterised by force, fraud, or coercion, is distinct in that the individuals involved are not "criminals" but rather victims of serious exploitation and abuse. However, this distinction is difficult to discern within the broader population of illegal immigrants, many of whom share similar backgrounds of hardship and desperation, creating a nuanced challenge for authorities tasked with upholding immigration laws while protecting vulnerable individuals. Traffickers skillfully exploit this ambiguity, instructing their victims to present as illegal immigrants, often even coaching them on responses to potential questioning. This strategy not only makes the trafficked individuals harder to identify but shields traffickers themselves from detection and prosecution, hiding the true nature of the abuse in plain sight.

The moment an immigrant is detained, law enforcement officials are often limited in their ability to fully investigate whether the individual is a trafficking victim. Resources, time, and protocols may simply not permit the intensive examination necessary to distinguish between an individual who has crossed borders seeking work and one who has been coerced, threatened, or forced into exploitative conditions. This lack of capacity to identify victims becomes a systemic barrier to protecting those who are trafficked. Traffickers rely on the fact that immigration protocols often prioritise swift processing, and in this setting, victims are rushed through the system without the chance for a deeper, trauma-informed screening that could reveal their exploitation. Detained immigrants are typically treated as violators of immigration law, often criminalised and processed for deportation, which increases the likelihood that victims of trafficking will slip through the cracks.

The challenge of identifying trafficked individuals among immigrants is further complicated by inadequate training and limited resources within law enforcement and immigration services. As explored in Chapter 5, corruption is a critical obstacle to anti-trafficking efforts, often involving bribed or complicit officials. Here, a similar challenge is posed by the sheer lack of training and support available to those on the frontlines of immigration enforcement. Many officials are simply not equipped to identify the subtle indicators of trafficking, nor are they trained to approach suspected victims with the sensitivity required. A victim of trafficking, for example, may display fear, provide contradictory statements, or struggle to disclose their experiences due to trauma, but without training, law enforcement may mistake these behaviours for evasiveness or uncooperativeness. In many instances, these indicators go unnoticed or are misunderstood, preventing officials from distinguishing between trafficked individuals and those who have entered a country illegally.

The line between an exploited migrant worker and a trafficking victim is exceedingly thin, and traffickers actively work to blur this line, manipulating the legal system to maintain control over their victims. In many cases, traffickers instruct victims on how to avoid drawing attention to their situation, perhaps by encouraging them to withhold details or lie about their working conditions. This creates a double layer of control: traffickers not only exploit victims physically and economically but also psychologically, reinforcing the idea that victims are criminals rather than individuals with rights. This is exacerbated by the structure of many legal systems, which struggle to balance punitive immigration enforcement with protections for vulnerable individuals, especially when traffickers are adept at coaching victims to avoid disclosure.

The result is a murky legal environment where exploitation becomes nearly indistinguishable from ordinary breaches of immigration law, leaving law enforcement with few practical tools for intervention. For instance, when immigration officers encounter individuals working in sectors commonly associated with trafficking, such as agriculture, construction, or domestic service, there may be little evidence to suggest the individual is anything other than an undocumented worker. Traffickers exploit these assumptions, placing victims in roles that appear typical for undocumented immigrants, masking any overt signs of trafficking. Without adequate legal frameworks and investigative resources, this ambiguity continues to prevent meaningful intervention.

Additionally, immigration officials often face the ethical dilemma of prioritising either strict immigration enforcement or victim protection. When law enforcement's primary role is defined by the removal of undocumented individuals, there is little incentive to pause and investigate the potential for trafficking. Moreover, if officials do identify signs of trafficking, there are frequently few resources available for victim assistance, which creates further ethical tension. Given these pressures, trafficked individuals risk being treated as violators rather than victims, reinforcing their vulnerabilities and leaving them in a position of continued exploitation.

Addressing these issues requires reform on multiple fronts. Immigration enforcement agencies must receive enhanced training in trauma-informed approaches, equipping officers to recognise signs of trafficking even within high-pressure and resource-constrained environments. Comprehensive victim identification protocols must be developed, ideally including standardised, non-punitive interview practices that allow victims to feel safe disclosing their circumstances. Cross-agency collaboration between immigration authorities and anti-trafficking units is essential, allowing specialised personnel to assist in complex cases where trafficking is suspected. By fostering an environment that prioritises victim identification, rather than simply enforcing immigration status, law enforcement can begin to dismantle the protective barriers traffickers rely on to continue their exploitation unchecked.

Ultimately, this intricate web of challenges underscores the urgent need for a holistic approach that balances immigration enforcement with a focus on the human rights of potential victims. Strengthening anti-trafficking protocols within immigration systems and providing law enforcement with the resources needed to identify trafficking victims, even among illegal immigrants, is essential to disrupt the cycle of exploitation and ensure that trafficking victims are not further victimised by the systems meant to protect them.

Law Enforcement and Policy Challenges

Effective law enforcement is essential to countering trafficking, yet Western authorities often struggle to protect trafficking victims who enter illegally. Legal ambiguity further exacerbates these challenges; while immigration authorities are tasked with controlling borders, anti-trafficking initiatives aim to safeguard victims, sometimes creating tension between immigration enforcement and victim protection. A lack of coordinated response allows traffickers to persist under the radar, shielded by overlapping or contradictory objectives.

In any robust anti-trafficking framework, the role of law enforcement is indispensable. Yet, in Western nations, particularly those with high volumes of migration, enforcing these anti-trafficking measures becomes complicated when victims enter through illegal channels. Traffickers know this well; they exploit both the bureaucratic divides between immigration enforcement and victim protection and the sometimes conflicting mandates within these agencies. Immigration enforcement is designed to protect borders and, in doing so, focuses on curbing illegal entry. This often places immigrants including trafficking victims under suspicion, resulting in detention, interrogation, and sometimes immediate deportation without assessing whether they may be victims of exploitation.

This conflict becomes particularly evident when immigration agencies and anti-trafficking organisations lack a collaborative or integrated approach. Law enforcement officers responsible for immigration control may not be trained in the nuanced identifiers of trafficking, which differ significantly from those related to typical illegal immigration cases. This gap creates what traffickers perceive as an opportunity: they know that a vulnerable individual if presented as an "illegal immigrant" rather than a victim, is less likely to receive sympathetic scrutiny. Victims are coached to feign ignorance or compliance, hiding signs of coercion or abuse to avoid any detection of trafficking. Such loopholes allow traffickers to continue their operations largely undisturbed, while authorities inadvertently miss crucial indicators of exploitation.

In Western nations, the conflation of trafficking and illegal immigration often forces authorities to choose between enforcement and assistance. This dichotomy can result in a "one size fits all" approach that disregards the nuance of each case, resulting in the deportation of trafficking victims who may need protection rather than punitive measures.

The institutional conflation of trafficking and illegal immigration creates a critical blind spot for Western authorities. While immigration officials are generally mandated to detain and deport those without legal status, anti-trafficking advocates insist on recognising and protecting victims, regardless of their means of entry. This clash of priorities means that, too often, trafficking victims are processed as illegal immigrants, subject to deportation rather than afforded the protections they require and deserve. The prevailing approach tends to default to punitive measures rather than investigative or protective actions. For individuals caught in the dragnet of immigration enforcement, this "one size fits all" strategy can strip away opportunities to escape from their traffickers and start anew.

Moreover, deporting a trafficking victim is not merely an administrative error; it can be a profound act of re-traumatisation. Victims who have undergone unimaginable abuse may be returned to the same environments and, in some cases, the same traffickers they initially fled. Their experiences are nullified by procedures that fail to distinguish between those complicit in immigration violations and those ensnared in trafficking rings. Without specialised intervention, victims often find themselves re-trafficked, re-entering the same vicious cycles of exploitation they once attempted to escape.

The framework of victim identification, as discussed in previous chapters, is inadequate when applied to undocumented immigrants. Law enforcement agents may not be trained to recognise the markers of trafficking, let alone the cultural or linguistic cues necessary to build trust with victims from diverse backgrounds.

The current frameworks for identifying victims of trafficking are largely based on an idealised scenario where victims willingly come forward, explain their situation, and seek protection. However, in the real world, particularly within undocumented immigrant populations, this scenario is rare. Victims are frequently isolated, culturally alienated, and fearful of law enforcement, making identification all the more challenging. Furthermore, traffickers often instil a deep-seated mistrust of authorities within their victims, warning them of deportation or even arrest if they attempt to seek help. This psychological manipulation, coupled with language barriers, prevents victims from articulating their plight.

As discussed in earlier chapters, indicators of trafficking can include signs of coercion, inconsistent personal narratives, fear of authority figures, and physical or emotional distress. However, these markers are nuanced and can be easily overlooked by law enforcement officials whose primary training focuses on identifying illegal immigration rather than exploitation. In the absence of clear training and structured guidelines, law enforcement personnel may unwittingly categorise a trafficking victim as a routine case of illegal immigration, missing vital signs of exploitation.

Moreover, cultural and linguistic barriers create an additional layer of complexity. Victims may come from diverse backgrounds, with distinct languages, customs, and forms of non-verbal communication. These differences make it challenging for untrained officials to interpret the subtle cues or fragmented disclosures that may reveal trafficking. In some cases, traffickers exploit cultural taboos or familial expectations that discourage open dialogue about exploitation, making it even harder for victims to come forward.

Inadequate Enforcement and the Cycle of Exploitation

The enforcement landscape in Western countries also faces issues beyond simply distinguishing trafficking victims from illegal immigrants; it grapples with systemic inefficiencies that allow traffickers to operate with minimal interference. While the threat of deportation looms over victims, actual consequences for traffickers are often minimal. Lax enforcement against trafficking networks due to limited resources, understaffing, or prioritisation of immigration over anti-trafficking measures creates a system where traffickers face little deterrent, emboldening them to continue exploiting vulnerable populations.

When traffickers feel secure in their operations, the cycle of exploitation perpetuates itself. They recruit new victims, reinforce existing control measures, and broaden their networks, confident in their immunity from serious legal repercussions. As a result, law enforcement inadvertently becomes part of a reactive system, dealing with the symptoms of trafficking rather than dismantling the structures that facilitate it. This cycle underscores the urgent need for a more nuanced approach one that goes beyond superficial immigration checks and embraces a proactive stance against traffickers themselves.

A Way Forward: Bridging the Divide

The divide between immigration enforcement and anti-trafficking protections is not an insurmountable one. Reframing the immigration narrative, from one of strict control to a balanced approach that incorporates both security and victim protection, may be key to bridging this divide. Specialised training, multilingual resources, and a more holistic understanding of trafficking indicators could transform the capabilities of immigration and law enforcement agencies alike. These efforts would require not only political will but also a willingness to view undocumented immigrants with a lens of compassion, recognising the very real possibility that they are victims in need of assistance, rather than criminals to be deported.

Coordinated multi-agency collaboration could further aid in reconciling the competing priorities within law enforcement, ensuring that neither border security nor victim protection is compromised. By recognising the unique vulnerabilities of undocumented migrants, authorities may yet forge a path forward that both respects the integrity of borders and upholds a commitment to human rights. Only through such concerted, cross-disciplinary efforts can we hope to dismantle the deeply ingrained systems that enable human trafficking to flourish in the shadow of migration.

Towards a Solution: Rethinking Policy to Combat Trafficking

Western immigration policies must evolve to address the realities of human trafficking. A dual approach that both secures borders and recognises the complexities of trafficking is essential. This could include enhanced training for immigration and law enforcement officers to differentiate between trafficking victims and illegal immigrants. Screening processes at border entries and within immigrant detention centres must integrate methodologies that identify trafficking indicators and safeguard those who might otherwise fall through the cracks.

The urgency for an evolved immigration policy framework stems from the realisation that traditional approaches often fail to capture the nuanced dynamics of human trafficking. In an ideal world, immigration enforcement and victim protection would operate hand in hand, yet these objectives frequently clash. Border security measures are primarily designed to curb illegal immigration, prioritising detention and deportation as responses. However, trafficking victims often fall within this population, obscured by the methods traffickers use to make them appear as illegal immigrants. By enhancing training specifically tailored to detect signs of trafficking, immigration officers can be equipped to distinguish between those unlawfully crossing borders for economic reasons and those forced or coerced into movement through trafficking.

This dual approach demands robust and ongoing training, especially as traffickers constantly adapt their methods to exploit systemic weaknesses. Traditional screening processes often focus on basic documentation or criminal records, missing behavioural cues and the subtle signs of coercion. Screening methods must evolve beyond mere paperwork to include psychological assessment, language support, and expertise in the tactics traffickers use. A comprehensive assessment can reveal indicators of exploitation, allowing victims to be redirected towards assistance rather than incarceration or deportation.

Partnerships between governments and non-governmental organisations (NGOs) play a crucial role in bridging these policy gaps. NGOs, with their expertise in handling trafficking cases and often greater freedom to operate on the ground, can offer invaluable insights into the nature of trafficking operations and the experiences of victims. Integrating their methodologies into immigration screening processes and providing victims with channels to confidentially report their exploitation would mark an important step forward in tackling this issue.

While NGOs have long been critical players in the fight against trafficking, their role has come under scrutiny due to concerns over ideological bias and financial dependencies. Many NGOs operate with a strong humanitarian ethos, which can sometimes lead to unintended consequences. For instance, NGOs advocating for open-border policies might inadvertently facilitate conditions that allow traffickers to exploit the influx of migrants. The absence of a strong, structured border allows traffickers to smuggle victims into countries with greater ease, increasing the burden on law enforcement who are often ill-prepared for the scale of trafficking operations.

Financial pressures also play a role. NGOs often depend on grants and donations, which can sometimes dictate their operational priorities and messaging. This dependency can create a situation where NGOs are hesitant to support more stringent border controls, even when these controls may be necessary to combat trafficking. Ideological commitments to unrestricted migration can sometimes overshadow the pressing need for a more balanced approach that considers both humanitarian and security imperatives. If NGOs are to serve as effective partners in the fight against trafficking, they must adopt a more nuanced stance that recognises the need for secure borders as a deterrent to traffickers.

A practical way forward would be to establish clearer protocols for collaboration between NGOs and government agencies. NGOs bring essential expertise in victim support, legal assistance, and cultural sensitivity, areas where law enforcement might lack proficiency. By integrating these strengths into border and immigration processes, victims could have access to trusted advocates who are attuned to the signs of trafficking and can offer pathways to protection, rather than punitive measures. This collaboration could include creating confidential reporting channels, where victims feel safe disclosing their experiences without fear of automatic deportation.

The Challenge of Open Border Policies and Law Enforcement Overwhelm

Open-border policies, which are often advocated by humanitarian groups and certain political movements, present another challenge in the fight against trafficking. While these policies aim to protect the rights of migrants, they can create environments ripe for exploitation. Traffickers use open borders as a cover, embedding their operations within the increased flow of individuals, making it harder for law enforcement to differentiate between genuine migrants and those being trafficked. As a result, law enforcement agencies are not only stretched thin but also find themselves in a reactive position, trying to address trafficking only after it has occurred rather than preventing it at the outset.

This overwhelm comes with significant consequences: traffickers often face minimal risk of interception or prosecution under such policies. When enforcement efforts are diluted by high volumes of immigration cases, traffickers operate with near impunity, confident that their victims will be processed as illegal immigrants and, likely, deported or detained without deeper investigation. The sheer volume of cases strains resources, diminishing the capacity for thorough screening and eroding public trust in the system's ability to protect vulnerable populations.

As such, the intersection of human trafficking and immigration presents one of the most formidable challenges within this global crisis. While anti-immigration policies are designed with security in mind, they must be tempered with awareness of the unintended consequences for those fleeing instability. Recognising and addressing the vulnerabilities that traffickers exploit within migrant populations offers an opportunity to redefine Western immigration policies, blending humanitarian protection with responsible border management.

Addressing trafficking within immigration policies is a delicate balance. Overly restrictive measures can trap genuine refugees and victims in limbo, fearing that reaching out for help could lead to their deportation. On the other hand, policies that are too lenient risk creating environments where traffickers flourish, exploiting open borders and inadequate enforcement mechanisms. Traffickers prey on instability and desperation, knowing that migrants fleeing conflict or economic hardship are often too fearful or financially constrained to resist or report their exploiters.

To achieve a more balanced policy, immigration systems could adopt flexible response mechanisms that adapt to the varied situations of trafficking victims. Screening for trafficking indicators should be standardised across Western nations, and protections for trafficking victims should be codified into law. For instance, establishing "safe harbours" within immigration law would allow victims to seek help without immediate risk of deportation, ensuring they are treated as survivors rather than offenders. Immigration policies should also integrate robust aftercare programs so that victims receive ongoing support as they transition out of exploitation and reintegrate into society.

If we are to dismantle trafficking networks and genuinely protect those at risk, we must focus not only on the traffickers but also on the structures and policies that inadvertently enable their insidious trade.

Tackling trafficking requires dismantling the socio-political structures that enable it. Policies that inadvertently shield traffickers by neglecting the needs of victims within immigration systems must be re-evaluated. In practical terms, this means not only enhancing security at borders but also ensuring that immigration and trafficking enforcement agencies are well-funded, well-coordinated, and supported by both governmental and non-governmental actors.

Addressing the ideological dimensions influencing policy decisions is also crucial. NGOs and policymakers must work within a pragmatic framework that acknowledges the necessity of border security as a protective measure. Only by addressing these structural gaps and ideological divides can we create an environment that both deters traffickers and genuinely aids victims. This approach will require a paradigm shift in how immigration is viewed, from a binary choice between open borders and restrictionism to a more nuanced stance that protects borders and people with equal commitment.

As such, a comprehensive anti-trafficking strategy must be multi-layered and collaborative, combining the strengths of law enforcement, NGOs, and victim support services. By reimagining immigration policies through the lens of trafficking prevention, the West can better address the dual objectives of border security and humanitarian protection. This approach holds promise not only in reducing trafficking incidents but also in fostering a more humane and effective immigration system that genuinely serves and protects those in need.

Chapter 9: The Psychological and Physical Toll: What Victims Endure

In this chapter, I turn to one of the most heart-wrenching aspects of human trafficking: the enduring trauma borne by its victims. The physical and psychological consequences of trafficking are catastrophic, tearing through the very fabric of a person's identity and well-being. Understanding these impacts goes to the heart of recognising why human trafficking is not merely a criminal enterprise, but a profound violation of human rights and dignity.

From relentless physical abuse, starvation, and deprivation, to the psychological torment of captivity and isolation, trafficking leaves indelible scars that often take years if not a lifetime to heal. This chapter aims to provide insight into the horrors that victims endure, exploring both their physical and mental suffering, with particular attention to the unique challenges faced by children and victims of sexual exploitation.

1. The Physical Consequences of Trafficking

The physical toll of human trafficking is visible and, for many victims, irreversible. Survivors often report prolonged periods of starvation and dehydration, conditions used by traffickers to control their captives and break their resistance. This starvation leaves victims with permanent damage to their bodies, weakening immune systems, stunting growth in children, and resulting in chronic ailments. In many cases, traffickers apply these methods in stages to ensure that their victims remain compliant, always on the verge of collapse but rarely in a state severe enough to attract outside attention.

Physical abuse is another devastating aspect of trafficking, manifesting in various forms depending on the type of exploitation. Victims of forced labour may endure gruelling, hazardous working conditions without proper equipment, leading to chronic injuries. The mining, agricultural, and manufacturing industries often subject trafficked individuals to toxic chemicals, extreme temperatures, and physically punishing labour, resulting in respiratory issues, severe lacerations, musculoskeletal problems, and in some cases, even amputations. In the sex trade, physical abuse takes on an even more heinous character. Survivors recount horrific stories of violence at the hands of both traffickers and clients, resulting in broken bones, internal injuries, and sexually transmitted infections. In both cases, untreated injuries lead to lifelong pain and disability.

The deprivation experienced by trafficked individuals is not limited to food and water; it extends to basic medical care and hygiene. Many trafficked persons are kept in unhygienic environments, without access to sanitary facilities or even clean clothing. This environment fosters the spread of infections and disease, compounding the misery of physical injury. Women, especially those forced into sexual exploitation, often suffer gynaecological injuries and complications from repeated sexual assault, compounded by a lack of medical attention. As a result, their bodies are ravaged by preventable illnesses, which many survivors struggle to manage even after escaping trafficking.

The Psychological Trauma of Trafficking

The physical injuries sustained by trafficking victims only scratch the surface of their suffering. The psychological toll of captivity and isolation is often more harrowing and enduring. Traffickers employ psychological manipulation techniques to maintain control, breaking down the mental defences of their victims through a systematic cycle of fear, dependency, and degradation. Survivors frequently describe their captivity as living in a perpetual state of terror, constantly aware of the violence that could be inflicted upon them if they attempted to escape or disobeyed orders.

Isolation is one of the most potent tools traffickers use to maintain control. Victims are often cut off from any external contact, confined to cramped, isolated spaces where they have no access to information about the outside world. This isolation erodes their sense of reality, rendering them increasingly dependent on their captors for survival. This psychological isolation is particularly effective with trafficked children, who lack the life experience to interpret their situation and often come to believe that their captors are the only people they can trust. By cutting victims off from society, traffickers strip away their sense of self and autonomy, creating a bond of dependency that is as powerful as physical chains.

Many trafficking survivors develop complex psychological conditions due to the abuse they endure. Post-traumatic stress disorder (PTSD) is widespread among survivors, manifesting as flashbacks, nightmares, and hypervigilance that persist long after they have escaped their captors. Depression, anxiety, and substance abuse are also common, as survivors seek any means of coping with their trauma. Victims who have been trafficked for extended periods often display symptoms of complex PTSD, a condition that involves dissociation, memory loss, and a deeply fractured sense of self. This trauma is not easily healed; for many, it persists throughout their lives, a constant reminder of the brutality they endured.

The Unique Trauma Faced by Child Victims

The trafficking of children is particularly egregious, as it inflicts irreversible damage on young, impressionable minds and bodies. Unlike adults, children often lack the emotional and psychological tools to process abuse, making them more susceptible to manipulation and long-term trauma. In previous chapters, I highlighted how traffickers exploit vulnerable populations, including children fleeing poverty, war, or abusive homes. These young victims are drawn into trafficking networks that see them as commodities to be sold and discarded.

Children trafficked for forced labour face gruelling conditions similar to adults, often worse because they lack the physical strength to withstand the tasks imposed on them. Many are coerced into work in agriculture, mining, or factory settings, where they are exposed to dangerous machinery, chemicals, and back-breaking labour, all while being deprived of education and nurturing experiences essential for healthy development. The resulting trauma from this experience deprives them not only of childhood but often of the capacity for trust and connection in later life.

The trauma endured by child victims of sexual exploitation is even more harrowing. These children are subjected to sexual abuse and exploitation daily, often beginning at a very young age. Their bodies are not developed to withstand such abuse, leading to serious physical injuries and complications that persist into adulthood. The psychological trauma is equally severe; young survivors of sexual exploitation often struggle with profound shame, guilt, and confusion, unable to reconcile the abuse they suffered with their developing sense of identity. Many of these children develop severe attachment issues, finding it difficult to form healthy relationships due to the violation of their basic trust in others.

As outlined in Chapter 7: *The Western Demand: Sex, Labour, and Exploitation*, the demand for trafficked children in certain sectors exacerbates this tragedy, creating a market that directly profits from the abuse of minors. Traffickers often ensure that these children never feel safe or in control, conditioning them to view exploitation as a norm rather than an aberration.

Long-Term Effects and the Path to Recovery

The physical and psychological toll of trafficking does not end with liberation. Many survivors face a long, complex road to recovery, as the trauma they have endured cannot be easily erased. Physical injuries often persist, sometimes requiring extensive medical interventions that many survivors cannot afford. Similarly, chronic illnesses contracted during captivity whether from forced labour or sexual exploitation may necessitate lifelong care, impacting survivors' ability to live fully independent lives.

Psychological recovery, too, is fraught with obstacles. Many survivors find it difficult to reintegrate into society, as they struggle with feelings of mistrust, shame, and isolation. PTSD is common, with victims suffering from flashbacks, nightmares, and severe anxiety, which can make even daily activities a source of distress. Survivors of trafficking often find it challenging to form relationships or secure stable employment, especially when they carry visible scars or criminal records from activities they were forced into.

The healing journey is made more difficult by societal stigma. Trafficking survivors frequently encounter discrimination or judgment, particularly if they were trafficked for sexual exploitation. Society's tendency to blame the victim adds a layer of trauma, making it difficult for survivors to regain a sense of normalcy. Rehabilitation programmes that address both the physical and mental needs of survivors are crucial, but they are not universally available and often fall short due to limited funding or inadequate understanding of the complex trauma associated with trafficking.

Challenges in Rehabilitation: The Role of Support Systems and Government Programmes

Efforts to support survivors of trafficking must be robust, comprehensive, and empathetic. However, the assistance available to survivors varies widely and is often inadequate. In many cases, survivors are offered only short-term relief, lacking the long-term psychological and financial support necessary to reintegrate successfully. As discussed in Chapter 5: *The Role of Corruption: How Governance and Law Enforcement Fail*, government systems meant to protect victims are often undermined by corruption or a lack of resources, leaving survivors without the safeguards they need.

Moreover, societal re-entry is especially difficult for foreign-born survivors. The intersection of immigration and trafficking, explored in Chapter 8: *Human Trafficking and Immigration: The Blurred Lines*, demonstrates how foreign nationals face unique obstacles, including deportation risks, language barriers, and a lack of family or community support. Without reliable support systems, these survivors are at risk of falling back into exploitation or developing substance abuse problems as a coping mechanism. For those who manage to escape or are rescued, the journey toward recovery is fraught with challenges. Many survivors find themselves in societies that lack the resources or understanding needed to support their unique needs. Physical injuries often require extensive medical treatment and rehabilitation, which can be inaccessible or prohibitively expensive. Even when medical care is available, survivors face additional hurdles as they struggle to navigate healthcare systems that may not be equipped to handle the specialised care they require.

Psychological recovery is even more complex. Many survivors enter therapy programs designed to treat trauma, yet traditional approaches are often insufficient for the type of sustained, complex trauma experienced by trafficked persons. Trauma-informed therapy, which acknowledges the profound and layered effects of abuse, is essential but frequently unavailable. Survivors often face social stigma, particularly those who have been trafficked for sexual exploitation, leading to further isolation. They may encounter discrimination when seeking employment, housing, or community acceptance, perpetuating the sense of alienation that trafficking ingrained in them.

The process of rebuilding a life shattered by trafficking is an arduous one, filled with setbacks and relapses. While some survivors find solace in support groups or advocacy work, others may struggle in silence, unable to escape the shadow of their past experiences. The lack of adequate support services, coupled with societal indifference, leaves many victims abandoned, bearing the weight of their trauma with little external assistance.

The Human Cost of Trafficking

In examining the physical and psychological toll of human trafficking, we uncover a deeper truth: trafficking is not merely a transgression against the law, but an assault on human dignity itself. This issue transcends legal definitions and crime statistics; it strikes at the very core of what it means to be human. To be trafficked is to be stripped of autonomy, subjected to profound suffering, and rendered invisible. The survivors of this trade bear more than the scars of abuse; they carry the burden of societal failure a failure to protect the vulnerable, to support those in need, and to recognise the inherent value of every human life.

The world often views human trafficking through the lens of criminal justice as a heinous act committed, a criminal apprehended, and justice served. But the reality is far more complex. Survivors do not simply emerge from their ordeals "rescued"; they carry the psychological and physical scars of their captivity, scars that may never fully heal. For many survivors, freedom from trafficking does not equate to freedom from the past. They face not only the challenges of rebuilding their lives but also the stigma, marginalisation, and mental anguish that linger. Society's failure lies not only in allowing trafficking to occur but in neglecting the survivors who need more than rescue they need understanding, support, and avenues to reclaim their humanity.

Trafficking as an Assault on Human Dignity

Human trafficking undermines the fundamental principle of human dignity, the idea that each person possesses intrinsic worth and deserves respect and autonomy. Trafficking reduces individuals to commodities, stripping them of their rights and freedoms, and treating them as instruments of profit. Survivors are forced into roles that negate their individuality and agency, whether as forced labourers, sexual objects, or domestic servants. Their personhood is eclipsed by the demands of those who exploit them, and this is more than a violation of law it is a violation of the human soul.

To endure trafficking is to suffer a profound loss of self. Victims often experience a complete deconstruction of their identity; they are not permitted to express their thoughts, their desires, or even their pain. In its place, traffickers impose a life that is not their own, a life ruled by fear and oppression. This assault on human dignity does not end when trafficking ends. Survivors emerge into a world where they must rebuild not only their external lives but also their inner sense of self-worth and humanity. By recognising the assault on dignity, we see that the crime of trafficking is not only one of exploitation but of annihilation of the human spirit.

The Burden of Societal Failure

Human trafficking exists because society, in many ways, permits it. Structural inequalities, economic desperation, lack of education, weak governance, and societal indifference all contribute to an environment where trafficking can thrive. Each trafficked individual represents a systemic failure a missed opportunity for protection, for intervention, for justice. For the victims, this societal failure adds a layer of trauma.

They have not only suffered abuse at the hands of traffickers but have also been betrayed by the very structures meant to protect them.

This failure is exacerbated when victims try to rebuild their lives and encounter barriers rather than support. Survivors often face systemic indifference or bureaucratic obstacles that hinder their recovery. Social services, when available, are often stretched thin, and ill-equipped to deal with the profound complexities of trafficking trauma. Law enforcement and healthcare providers may lack training in how to support survivors sensitively, and communities may regard these individuals with suspicion or even blame. Thus, survivors are repeatedly let down, often left isolated and vulnerable, carrying the dual burden of personal trauma and societal abandonment.

Addressing human trafficking requires acknowledging this societal complicity. Until society recognises the structural conditions that allow trafficking to flourish and fails to support those affected by it, the cycle will continue. It is only through collective responsibility and a commitment to root out trafficking's causes and support its survivors that we can hope to rectify these failures.

Trauma as a Catalyst for Urgency and Action

Understanding the trauma of trafficking survivors is essential not only for crafting effective policies and interventions but also for igniting a sense of urgency within society to address this crisis. The horrific experiences endured by trafficked individuals are not distant realities that affect only the vulnerable or marginalised; they represent a moral and ethical crisis that affects us all. The existence of trafficking within our borders, across our communities, and within the supply chains of products we consume is an indictment of our collective apathy and ignorance.

The trauma endured by survivors serves as a sobering reminder of the stakes involved in combating this heinous trade. Every day that trafficking persists, countless individuals are subject to unthinkable suffering. When we view trafficking through the lens of survivors' trauma, we see not a distant issue, but an immediate crisis that demands action. Recognising the depth of this trauma compels us to act not out of obligation, but out of empathy, urgency, and moral conviction. Only when society fully comprehends the agony inflicted on trafficking victims will there be a collective will to prevent future exploitation.

Beyond Criminal Justice: A Holistic Approach

As I reflect on the broader themes of this book, it becomes evident that human trafficking cannot be addressed solely through criminal justice. While law enforcement plays a crucial role in dismantling trafficking networks and prosecuting perpetrators, a criminal justice approach alone fails to address the root causes and lasting impact on survivors. Trafficking is not a crime that can simply be eradicated by arresting a few offenders; it is a complex social issue that requires a comprehensive, multi-layered approach.

To truly combat trafficking, society must adopt a holistic response that includes education, economic empowerment, mental health support, and legal reform. Prevention initiatives should aim to address the vulnerabilities that traffickers exploit, such as poverty, lack of education, and unstable communities. Rehabilitation programs for survivors must go beyond basic shelter and medical care; they should include trauma-informed therapy, job training, and community integration efforts. Furthermore, public awareness campaigns are essential to reduce the demand for trafficked labour and services, thereby striking at the economic incentives that drive trafficking networks.

Efforts to combat human trafficking must also include the voices of survivors. Those who have lived through this experience offer invaluable insights into the conditions that enable trafficking and the challenges of recovery. Policies and programs informed by survivors' perspectives are not only more effective but also restore dignity and agency to those who have been silenced. This survivor-centred approach to anti-trafficking efforts acknowledges that the path to healing is as important as the act of rescue itself.

A Call to Action: Restoring Dignity and Humanity

This journey toward understanding the trauma of trafficking is, ultimately, a call to action one that demands empathy, dedication, and an unwavering commitment to restoring the dignity of those who have suffered in silence. Society's response to human trafficking should not end with rescue; it must continue with support, advocacy, and a concerted effort to ensure survivors are not forgotten. We must not only confront traffickers but also challenge the apathy and complacency that allow trafficking to persist.

In the chapters that follow, I will explore potential avenues for reform and rehabilitation, considering how society can better respond to the needs of trafficking survivors and prevent future exploitation. This exploration will include practical steps such as policy recommendations, best practices for trauma-informed care, and strategies for raising awareness. At the heart of these efforts is a commitment to restoring humanity to those who have been dehumanised, recognising that healing from trafficking involves more than physical freedom it involves reclaiming one's identity, dignity, and right to a life unshackled by trauma.

The fight against human trafficking is not only a battle against crime; it is a battle for human rights, compassion, and justice. Addressing trafficking is not merely about punishing perpetrators; it is about changing societal norms, creating systems that protect the vulnerable, and fostering a culture that values every human life. By acknowledging the trauma of trafficking survivors, we take the first step toward a world where such exploitation is no longer tolerated, and where the dignity of every person is upheld as an inviolable truth.

Chapter 10: The Legal Framework: International and Domestic Responses

In examining the legal structures aimed at combating human trafficking, one encounters a complex tapestry of international conventions, regional agreements, and national legislation. Together, they form a framework designed to protect victims, prevent trafficking, and prosecute offenders. However, while comprehensive in scope, this legal landscape often reveals gaps in enforcement, challenges in jurisdictional cooperation, and varying levels of commitment among countries. Despite the existence of a multitude of international instruments and domestic laws across jurisdictions, a question persists: Are these laws effective in shielding victims and bringing traffickers to justice?

In answering this, I will conduct an in-depth analysis of key international instruments, such as the United Nations Protocol to Prevent, Suppress and Punish Trafficking in Persons, especially Women and Children (commonly known as the Palermo Protocol), alongside specific national laws in the United States and Europe. This chapter critically evaluates their strengths and limitations, along with the myriad challenges in enforcement, from insufficient victim protections to prosecutorial gaps. Drawing from the insights of previous chapters, I explore how these legal frameworks intersect with the exploitative networks discussed, the vulnerabilities traffickers manipulate, and the corrosive impact of systemic corruption.

Key International Instruments in Anti-Trafficking Legislation

The international legal framework governing anti-trafficking efforts is shaped primarily by conventions and protocols that compel states to adopt stringent national legislation. One of the most prominent of these instruments is the **United Nations Protocol to Prevent,**

Suppress and Punish Trafficking in Persons, especially Women and Children (2000), commonly known as the **Palermo Protocol**. Established under the broader **United Nations Convention against Transnational Organised Crime**, the Palermo Protocol obliges signatories to criminalise all forms of human trafficking, adopt measures to protect trafficking victims, and enhance international cooperation in trafficking prevention and enforcement. Article 5 of the Protocol mandates the criminalisation of trafficking in persons, compelling state parties to address this offence within their domestic legal systems.

The Palermo Protocol is a landmark in anti-trafficking efforts, representing the first time trafficking was defined on an international scale with a clear framework for prevention and victim support. Yet, its efficacy is inherently limited by the lack of binding enforcement mechanisms. While it provides a blueprint, actual implementation is left to individual nations, with significant disparities in execution. For instance, some states lack the resources or political will to enforce anti-trafficking measures, especially in regions plagued by corruption, which allows trafficking networks to operate with relative impunity a topic examined in *Chapter 5: The Role of Corruption: How Governance and Law Enforcement Fail*.

Additionally, the **Universal Declaration of Human Rights (UDHR)**, though not a legal mandate, establishes a fundamental principle in Article 4, prohibiting all forms of slavery and servitude. The **International Covenant on Civil and Political Rights (ICCPR)** reinforces this prohibition, emphasising individual freedom from exploitation and involuntary servitude. These documents provide a moral and legal foundation, underscoring the global commitment to ending trafficking, yet lack direct mechanisms to compel state compliance.

The **ILO Convention 29 on Forced Labour (1930)** and its **Protocol of 2014** are other critical instruments that focus specifically on forced labour, a key component of human trafficking. The 1930 Convention, with nearly universal ratification, mandates that state parties eliminate forced labour in all forms, while the 2014 Protocol reinforces these obligations with additional victim protection measures, including compensation and rehabilitation support. However, gaps remain, particularly in implementing forced labour protections for migrant populations, as highlighted in *Chapter 8: Human Trafficking and Immigration: The Blurred Lines.*

Regional instruments such as the **Council of Europe Convention on Action against Trafficking in Human Beings (2005)** expand on the Palermo Protocol by establishing a human rights-focused approach to trafficking, mandating that member states offer victims access to justice, compensation, and protection. This Convention takes a comprehensive view, acknowledging the role of socio-economic factors and discrimination in perpetuating trafficking. Nevertheless, enforcement is inconsistent among member states, with significant variation in resources allocated to victim support and prosecutorial initiatives.

National Legislative Responses: The United States and European Examples

Nationally, countries like the United States and European nations have introduced legislation to address trafficking within their jurisdictions. The **Trafficking Victims Protection Act (TVPA) of 2000** and its subsequent reauthorisations serve as the cornerstone of U.S. anti-trafficking efforts. The TVPA creates a three-tier system focused on "prosecution, protection, and prevention," establishing harsh penalties for traffickers while mandating victim services, such as immigration relief and financial assistance. Moreover, it introduced the **TIP (Trafficking in Persons) Report**, which ranks countries based on their anti-trafficking efforts, exerting diplomatic pressure on nations failing to address trafficking adequately.

Despite these legal provisions, enforcement of the TVPA remains inconsistent. State and local agencies often struggle with resource limitations and inter-agency coordination, allowing traffickers to exploit legal gaps. This fragmentation is exacerbated in cases where trafficking intersects with immigration laws, as described in *Chapter 8*. The U.S. legal system frequently prioritises border enforcement over victim protection, resulting in a punitive approach toward trafficked migrants, who are often treated as illegal immigrants rather than victims, a consequence of complex and sometimes conflicting laws.

In Europe, anti-trafficking legislation varies by country but is shaped significantly by **Directive 2011/36/EU on Preventing and Combating Trafficking in Human Beings and Protecting its Victims**. This Directive obliges EU member states to adopt a harmonised definition of trafficking, establish protections for victims, and create effective prosecutorial pathways. It requires a victim-centred approach, ensuring that trafficked individuals have access to legal support, safe housing, and healthcare. Yet, as with the Palermo Protocol, practical implementation varies. Some EU countries have strong anti-trafficking laws but struggle with enforcement due to limited funding, insufficient training for law enforcement, and societal biases against trafficking victims, particularly those involved in forced labour or the sex industry, as discussed in *Chapter 7: The Western Demand: Sex, Labour, and Exploitation*.

Countries like Germany and the Netherlands, for example, have enacted comprehensive anti-trafficking laws within the framework of the EU Directive, yet they continue to grapple with high trafficking rates. Corruption, language barriers, and varying levels of social services make enforcement a constant challenge. Conversely, Nordic countries such as Sweden have adopted the **Nordic Model** in their approach to the sex industry, criminalising the purchase of sex but not the individuals providing it, thereby aiming to reduce demand. Although this model has shown some success, it remains controversial and is criticised for driving trafficking further underground, complicating identification and prosecution efforts.

The Complexities of Enforcement: Barriers and Gaps

One of the most pervasive challenges in the legal fight against trafficking lies in the enforcement of existing laws. Legal provisions are only as effective as their implementation, and traffickers are adept at navigating the gaps within this complex framework. Trafficking networks, as described in *Chapter 4: The Machinery of Trafficking*, exploit differences in legal protections and enforcement practices across borders, often moving victims through jurisdictions with weaker laws or less robust policing. Corruption exacerbates these challenges, allowing traffickers to bribe officials, evade detection, and manipulate victims into silence.

Furthermore, international cooperation remains an ongoing hurdle. The *extraterritorial jurisdiction* clause in the Palermo Protocol allows countries to prosecute their nationals for trafficking offences committed abroad, but this principle is rarely applied due to diplomatic complexities and varying national interests. Moreover, the rise of technology, as discussed in *Chapter 6: The Digital Age: How Technology Fuels Human Trafficking*, has introduced new challenges in prosecuting traffickers who utilise encrypted platforms, dark web forums, and cryptocurrencies, all of which enable them to operate with anonymity across borders.

A lack of consistent victim protection also undermines enforcement efforts. Though the Palermo Protocol, TVPA, and EU Directive all include victim-protection provisions, many countries lack the infrastructure or resources to support trafficked individuals adequately. This failure is particularly harmful to victims of forced labour and sexual exploitation, who, as discussed in *Chapter 9: The Psychological and Physical Toll*, face immense psychological and physical challenges in attempting to rebuild their lives. Without appropriate legal, psychological, and financial assistance, these victims are often unable or unwilling to participate in legal proceedings, further reducing the chances of successful prosecution against their traffickers.

The Need for Comprehensive Reform

The current legal framework represents significant progress in the fight against human trafficking, yet it remains insufficient to address the global scale and complexities of the crime. Reforms must focus on closing the gaps in international cooperation, enhancing victim protections, and providing robust, well-funded enforcement mechanisms. A stronger commitment to multilateral collaboration, coupled with dedicated resources for victim support, would enhance the efficacy of these laws. Furthermore, integrating anti-corruption measures into anti-trafficking frameworks is crucial to preventing traffickers from exploiting weaknesses within legal and governmental systems.

Ultimately, the legal response to human trafficking requires a concerted, global effort to address not only the symptoms of trafficking but also its root causes, as discussed throughout this book. Only by tackling systemic issues such as the demand for trafficked individuals, corruption, and the vulnerabilities that traffickers exploit can the international community hope to dismantle the trafficking networks that continue to thrive within the gaps of this fragmented legal landscape.

The International Framework: Conventions and Protocols

The international community has long recognised human trafficking as a global crisis requiring a collaborative response. At the forefront is the United Nations' Palermo Protocol, adopted in 2000, which serves as the foundation for international anti-trafficking efforts. This protocol represents a milestone in recognising trafficking as a form of organised crime and aims to foster international cooperation in the prosecution of traffickers, protection of victims, and prevention of trafficking.

The Palermo Protocol was ground-breaking in defining human trafficking, outlining victim protections, and establishing penalties for trafficking-related offences. It requires signatory countries to adopt national legislation to meet these standards, a provision which has spurred many nations to enact or amend anti-trafficking laws. However, despite its widespread adoption, implementation remains inconsistent. The protocol, while strong in scope, lacks enforcement mechanisms to ensure compliance, relying on national governments to act in a reality that leaves enforcement vulnerable to local corruption and inadequate resourcing, as discussed in *Chapter 5: The Role of Corruption: How Governance and Law Enforcement Fail.*

Regional Instruments: The European Context

Europe has long served as both a destination and transit point for trafficking victims, making the need for regional action imperative. The European Union introduced the Directive 2011/36/EU on preventing and combating trafficking in human beings and protecting its victims, which mandates a victim-centred approach and focuses on victim identification, assistance, and protection. The Council of Europe's Convention on Action against Trafficking in Human Beings complements these efforts, emphasising the role of human rights in anti-trafficking laws. Both instruments represent a coordinated European approach, but they are not without shortcomings.

Despite the EU's comprehensive framework, enforcement is uneven across member states, with some countries enforcing stringent penalties and victim protections, while others struggle with implementation. The inconsistency weakens the overall effectiveness of the directive and creates gaps in which traffickers can operate relatively unchecked, particularly in countries that serve as gateways to the EU. Corruption, inadequate training for law enforcement, and limited resources in some countries further hinder implementation, especially in nations bordering trafficking hotspots, as discussed in *Chapter 2: The Routes to Exploitation* and *Chapter 4: The Machinery of Trafficking*. Additionally, complex immigration systems, as outlined in *Chapter 8: Human Trafficking and Immigration: The Blurred Lines*, have inadvertently made it challenging for victim identification and protection efforts to work effectively in practice.

Domestic Legislation: The United States Approach

In the United States, the Trafficking Victims Protection Act (TVPA) of 2000, and its subsequent reauthorisations, form the backbone of federal anti-trafficking efforts. The TVPA establishes severe penalties for traffickers and provides avenues for victim support, including the issuance of temporary visas for foreign victims willing to cooperate with law enforcement. The act also mandates the annual Trafficking in Persons (TIP) Report, which ranks countries based on their efforts to combat trafficking a diplomatic tool intended to pressure governments into compliance.

While the TVPA represents a robust legal response, practical enforcement is again hampered by challenges, particularly at state and local levels. Coordination across jurisdictions remains inconsistent, and traffickers exploit legal ambiguities, shifting tactics to evade prosecution. Furthermore, despite legislative protections, trafficking victims are often treated as criminals, especially when trafficking is intertwined with illegal immigration a complexity discussed extensively in *Chapter 8*. This punitive approach undermines victim protection, with victims either fearful of or mistrustful towards authorities, which discourages cooperation in prosecuting traffickers.

The Role of Enforcement: Gaps and Barriers

One of the most persistent issues in the legal response to human trafficking is enforcement. As outlined in *Chapter 5*, corruption within law enforcement and government agencies severely undermines the efficacy of anti-trafficking laws. Even where national legislation is strong, traffickers exploit officials willing to turn a blind eye in exchange for financial incentives, as well as convoluted legal systems that make enforcement difficult.

Moreover, the structures of organised crime, as discussed in *Chapter 4*, enable traffickers to operate across borders, circumventing national laws by exploiting weak jurisdictions or corruption within source countries. Border control is often the first point of failure, as corrupt or under-resourced officials allow traffickers to transport victims across borders unimpeded. Here, the inherent limitations of national enforcement clash with the transnational nature of trafficking, creating significant enforcement gaps.

The problem is further compounded by inconsistencies in victim protection. Many countries fail to meet the Palermo Protocol's mandate for victim protection, with victims often facing re-victimisation within the legal system. Those trafficked for forced labour or sexual exploitation, as outlined in *Chapter 7*, face the additional burden of proving victim status, a daunting requirement given the trauma and control methods traffickers use to silence and intimidate them, which is covered in detail in *Chapter 9: The Psychological and Physical Toll*.

Assessing Victim-Centred Approaches: A Critical View

The concept of a victim-centred approach is enshrined in almost every major anti-trafficking law or convention, and yet, practical applications frequently fall short. Victims face numerous obstacles in accessing support services, and there is often a reluctance among law enforcement to prioritise victim welfare over criminal prosecution. In reality, many trafficking victims continue to be treated as criminals, particularly in immigration contexts where trafficking is interwoven with illegal border crossings, as discussed in *Chapter 8*.

Child victims and those trafficked for sexual exploitation are among the most vulnerable, as highlighted in *Chapter 9*. The long-term psychological impact of trafficking, combined with a lack of adequate mental health and reintegration services, often leaves these victims struggling to reclaim their lives, and the legal system offers limited remedies. Legislation, while setting forth protective measures, is often reactive rather than proactive, focusing on criminalising traffickers instead of addressing the root causes of trafficking or offering substantial aid for rehabilitation.

The Path Forward: Reforming Anti-Trafficking Frameworks

A genuine shift toward a victim-centred approach in combating human trafficking requires a holistic, rights-based model that prioritises the rehabilitation, security, and dignity of trafficking survivors. This vision demands far more than symbolic legislative gestures; it necessitates real investment in support services that include safe housing, legal aid, medical care, psychological support, and reintegration assistance. In the current landscape, these vital resources are underfunded and often inaccessible to many victims, especially in jurisdictions that lack a coordinated national strategy.

Training for law enforcement is equally critical, as officers are frequently the first point of contact for trafficking survivors. Without specialised training to recognise trafficking indicators and understand the nuanced needs of victims, law enforcement officials may inadvertently criminalise survivors often treating them as illegal immigrants or offenders rather than vulnerable individuals in need of protection. This can deter victims from coming forward, out of fear of arrest or deportation, a significant barrier that underscores the need for widespread reforms aimed at shifting law enforcement's focus from prosecution to protection.

Furthermore, open-border policies, sanctuary city declarations, and insufficient policing resources have compounded these challenges, inadvertently creating conditions that traffickers exploit with devastating efficiency. While sanctuary cities aim to protect immigrants from federal immigration enforcement, they can also inadvertently shield traffickers who exploit these policies to avoid detection. Trafficking networks manipulate the complexities of immigration policies, using sanctuary cities as havens where they can operate under reduced scrutiny, which allows them to integrate trafficked individuals into local economies and evade law enforcement. Similarly, the underfunding of police forces, coupled with the overwhelming demands placed on them by rising trafficking cases, creates gaps that traffickers leverage to evade justice.

Open Borders and Sanctuary City Policies: Exacerbating Vulnerabilities to Trafficking

While open-border policies in the United States and parts of Western Europe are often rooted in humanitarian ideals, they have unintentionally created new vulnerabilities that traffickers exploit with precision. Open-border policies mean that large, often unvetted, migrant populations cross borders, including vulnerable individuals who traffickers easily prey upon. Migrants are promised false opportunities in destination countries, only to find themselves coerced into forced labour, sex work, or other exploitative practices upon arrival. In the absence of rigorous checks, traffickers move victims across borders under the guise of migration, and border authorities lack the resources or protocols to differentiate trafficked individuals from other migrants effectively.

Sanctuary city policies, while well-intentioned, further complicate anti-trafficking efforts by creating legal "grey zones" where cooperation between local law enforcement and federal immigration agencies is restricted. Traffickers exploit this lack of coordination to shield their operations within these cities, moving victims into areas where local police have limited authority or willingness to collaborate with federal immigration enforcement. In the United States, cities such as San Francisco, New York, and Chicago have declared themselves sanctuary cities, which limits immigration enforcement and allows traffickers to operate with less fear of prosecution or deportation, as these policies are frequently associated with a general reluctance to engage with federal authorities on immigration issues.

Furthermore, the United States **Trafficking Victims Protection Act (TVPA)**, though progressive in its structure, is rendered less effective in these cities, where traffickers and victims often remain hidden within informal or illegal labour sectors. In sanctuary cities, trafficking cases that would normally be referred to federal authorities may remain in the local jurisdiction, where funding and resources for specialised anti-trafficking efforts are limited, creating additional impediments to prosecuting traffickers and identifying victims.

Underfunded Law Enforcement: The Resource Gap in Anti-Trafficking Operations

Effective enforcement of anti-trafficking laws relies heavily on the availability of resources to conduct proactive investigations, provide victim support, and prosecute traffickers to the fullest extent. Yet, law enforcement agencies tasked with combatting trafficking are often critically underfunded, with limited manpower and tools to track, investigate, and dismantle complex trafficking networks. This financial constraint is especially apparent in cases of cross-border trafficking, which requires costly surveillance operations, language expertise, and international cooperation that many local and even federal law enforcement agencies cannot afford.

The **United Nations Office on Drugs and Crime (UNODC)** and the **Global Report on Trafficking in Persons** consistently stress the need for adequate funding to strengthen anti-trafficking operations and victim support. However, without dedicated budgets, law enforcement agencies in countries like the United States face significant challenges. The focus often shifts to high-profile trafficking cases, leaving smaller but no less damaging operations unchecked, which creates a fertile environment for traffickers who understand and exploit these enforcement gaps.

Underfunding is particularly severe in rural and suburban areas, where trafficking is prevalent but largely unnoticed due to a lack of specialised resources. In under-resourced areas, police may lack training and personnel to handle trafficking cases effectively. This disparity in resources allows traffickers to target low-income and rural communities, operating with minimal risk of detection. Additionally, in urban areas with high levels of gang and organised crime activity, such as Los Angeles or Chicago, trafficking investigations are frequently sidelined by competing priorities within law enforcement agencies. Traffickers know this and take advantage, embedding their networks in these areas, aware that law enforcement has neither the personnel nor funding to mount sustained investigations against them.

The Need for Rigorous Reform and Dedicated Victim Protection

These policy and resource-related challenges point to the necessity of structural reforms that prioritise victim protection and improve anti-trafficking enforcement. The **Palermo Protocol** mandates that countries adopt measures to protect and assist victims of trafficking, yet without sufficient funding and a supportive policy environment, these provisions remain aspirational rather than operational. Reform efforts must include:

1. **Enhanced Funding for Anti-Trafficking Units**: Substantial federal and local investments in specialised anti-trafficking units are essential to address the resource deficits that allow traffickers to evade justice. This includes providing officers with the necessary technology, additional personnel, and the ability to collaborate with other agencies effectively.

2. **Expanded Training for Law Enforcement**: Anti-trafficking training that goes beyond basic law enforcement to include victim psychology, legal protections, and trafficking-specific investigative methods is crucial. Law enforcement officers need to be equipped not only with legal tools but also with an understanding of how to approach victims with sensitivity and respect, ensuring that they are seen as individuals requiring protection rather than potential criminals.

3. **Policy Reforms on Sanctuary Cities and Immigration Protocols**: Policies need to strike a balance between protecting the rights of migrants and creating loopholes that traffickers exploit. Establishing controlled collaboration between sanctuary city law enforcement and federal immigration officials would allow authorities to more effectively identify and assist trafficking victims while maintaining the protective ethos of sanctuary policies.

4. **Dedicated Victim Support Services**: Legislation alone

cannot address the complexities of human trafficking without robust support for survivors. Governments should mandate funding for shelters, legal aid, mental health services, and job training programmes to aid in the full recovery and reintegration of survivors into society.

Bridging the Gap Between Legal Provisions and Practical Outcomes

While current frameworks such as the TVPA, Palermo Protocol, and national legislation in various Western countries mark significant progress, they are undermined by policy gaps, enforcement limitations, and inadequate victim support. The exacerbating effects of open-border policies, sanctuary city protections, and chronic underfunding of law enforcement create a modern environment where traffickers operate with relative impunity. As human trafficking becomes increasingly sophisticated, anti-trafficking strategies must evolve, backed by adequate funding, policy reform, and a commitment to true victim-centred protection.

For the law to serve as a genuine tool against trafficking, it must be adapted to address the systemic weaknesses traffickers exploit. Only through rigorous reform, targeted investment in law enforcement, and unwavering dedication to victim protection can these laws become the effective mechanisms they were intended to be in combatting one of the gravest human rights violations of our time.

Chapter 11: Survivor Stories: Resilience in the Face of Horror

In exploring the landscape of human trafficking, one cannot simply rely on statistics, legal frameworks, or even the mechanics of organised crime to truly understand the profound human impact of this crisis. Behind every figure lies a face, a name, a story of trauma, resilience, and, for many survivors, a harrowing journey towards recovery and self-reclamation. This chapter is dedicated to bringing forward the voices of those who have endured the horrors of trafficking and emerged from it – scarred, changed, yet resilient.

Through personal testimonies, this chapter will add a human dimension to the preceding discussions, from the complexities of trafficking routes detailed in Chapter 2 to the in-depth analysis of victim profiles in Chapter 3, and the psychological and physical toll explored in Chapter 9. By hearing directly from survivors, we gain insight into not only the trauma they have suffered but also their remarkable resilience and the myriad challenges they face in rebuilding their lives in Western societies that often struggle to understand, let alone accommodate, their needs.

The Stories that Demand to Be Heard

Each story of survival is unique, yet common threads often emerge. The narratives range from those who were forced into the sex trade to individuals coerced into gruelling labour with little hope of escape. Survivors I interviewed spoke of promises that initially seemed to offer salvation, hope, and economic opportunity, only to find themselves ensnared in a web of exploitation. Their experiences reflect the deception and brutality highlighted in Chapter 4, where organised crime networks capitalise on the vulnerabilities of the disenfranchised, and in Chapter 8, which discusses the exploitation of migrant populations.

In recounting their experiences, survivors described the relentless physical and psychological toll they endured – themes closely examined in Chapter 9. Many were kept in inhumane conditions, often subjected to violence, starvation, and deprivation. For some, the ordeal left them physically debilitated, with chronic injuries, malnutrition, or illnesses that went untreated. Psychologically, the scars are perhaps even deeper, with many survivors facing post-traumatic stress disorder (PTSD), anxiety, depression, and a long road towards emotional healing.

Navigating the Path to Recovery

The path to recovery for trafficking survivors is often fraught with obstacles. Many survivors speak of an intense distrust of authority figures, a consequence of the betrayal they experienced from individuals meant to uphold the law, as discussed in Chapter 5 on the role of corruption. Some were trafficked by figures of authority in their homelands, while others faced indifference or even complicity from officials in destination countries. This betrayal leaves lasting trauma, complicating survivors' ability to trust those trying to help them.

Western countries, where many survivors ultimately find refuge, often lack the specialised resources and support structures needed to address the complex trauma associated with trafficking. While some countries provide shelter, legal support, and basic healthcare, the psychological services necessary to truly help survivors heal are often inadequate. Many survivors find themselves navigating an unfamiliar system alone, with little access to mental health professionals trained to address trauma rooted in such extreme circumstances.

Survivors from diverse backgrounds, who came to the West for safety and recovery, face the additional challenge of cultural dissonance. They are often left isolated within the communities they hoped would offer solace. Additionally, navigating immigration laws can feel like another form of captivity, as bureaucratic obstacles force survivors to remain in limbo, unable to rebuild their lives due to uncertain legal status or the constant threat of deportation. These challenges were outlined in Chapter 8, where I discussed how immigration policies in the West, while aimed at preventing illegal entry, inadvertently create vulnerabilities that traffickers exploit, leaving survivors stuck in an institutional labyrinth.

The Importance of Resilience and Self-Reclamation

The strength and resilience shown by survivors are as remarkable as the trauma they have endured. Despite the obstacles, many survivors find a way to regain control over their lives, piecing together fragments of identity that traffickers sought to strip away. For many, this journey is neither linear nor easy. It is a continual struggle of self-reclamation, one that defies simple categorisation as "recovery" or "healing." Recovery is often a lifelong process, marked by periods of progress and regression.

Through the accounts of those who have rebuilt their lives, I observed that resilience takes many forms. For some, it lies in reclaiming control over their narratives – telling their stories not as passive victims but as individuals who survived unspeakable experiences and emerged with their spirits intact. This empowerment is not just therapeutic for survivors; it also acts as a profound statement against the traffickers who sought to erase their autonomy and humanity.

Yet even the most resilient survivors encounter institutional barriers that challenge their newfound autonomy. These hurdles often stem from inadequacies in Western legal systems discussed in Chapter 10, where well-intentioned laws aimed at protecting victims fail to accommodate the real needs of survivors. From the absence of comprehensive psychological care to restrictive work permits that prevent financial independence, the disconnect between legal frameworks and survivor needs is stark. Survivors frequently become entangled in bureaucratic webs that inhibit their ability to move forward – a painful irony after escaping the constraints of trafficking itself.

Survivor Testimonies as a Call to Action

These stories demand more than mere empathy; they necessitate a societal and structural response that extends beyond compassionate words or sympathetic gestures. The harrowing experiences shared by survivors highlight an urgent need for actionable change policies, frameworks, and a shift in societal consciousness that recognises the humanity behind every survivor's story. Acknowledging survivors is not enough; their voices must catalyse a restructuring of the systems that allowed their exploitation to occur in the first place.

Understanding these survivor experiences is essential for dismantling the multi-layered structures that facilitate trafficking. Corruption, economic demand, and systemic loopholes together create an environment where traffickers can exploit vulnerable populations with relative impunity. As discussed in previous chapters, corruption exists in all stages of trafficking: recruitment, transport, and even law enforcement. Corrupt officials, whether in source, transit, or destination countries, are frequently complicit, accepting bribes or turning a blind eye to traffickers' activities. Survivor accounts often reveal the tragic reality that, in many cases, they were betrayed not only by traffickers but also by those meant to protect them. Their testimonies underscore the necessity of anti-corruption measures, international accountability, and transparent governance in the fight against trafficking.

Yet corruption alone does not explain the prevalence of trafficking; demand in Western markets plays a critical role. Trafficking is, at its core, an economic transaction. It is driven by the desire for cheap labour, services, and, most disturbingly, exploitative sexual industries that benefit from trafficking victims. Chapter 7 explored how certain sectors, including agriculture, domestic work, and the sex trade, thrive on trafficked individuals who are often paid far below legal wage standards, denied basic rights, and forced to live in conditions unfit for human beings. Survivor testimonies highlight the grim reality that this demand is not an abstract issue it is a lived horror, where the exploitation is real, immediate, and often in plain sight. For those who have endured trafficking, knowing that their suffering served to fulfil Western demand compounds their trauma, making the need for a survivor-centred response all the more pressing.

The Need for a Survivor-Centred Approach

A survivor-centred approach recognises that the well-being and empowerment of trafficking survivors should be paramount in anti-trafficking efforts. Too often, policies are designed with prosecutorial or political objectives in mind, relegating survivors' needs to a secondary consideration. This approach not only fails to provide adequate support to survivors but can also result in their re-traumatisation, as they are treated as mere witnesses in legal proceedings rather than individuals deserving of holistic support.

In a survivor-centred framework, survivors' physical, psychological, and legal needs are addressed comprehensively, prioritising their recovery over any legal gains that may come from their cooperation as witnesses. Such an approach includes accessible mental health services, culturally competent support workers, and a pathway to legal residency and employment enabling survivors to rebuild their lives with dignity. When survivors are genuinely supported and empowered, they are more likely to regain agency over their lives, leading not only to personal healing but also to a broader cultural shift in how trafficking survivors are perceived and treated.

The Role of Survivor Voices in Societal Change

For many survivors, reclaiming their voices is an act of resilience and empowerment. By sharing their experiences, they confront not only personal trauma but also the broader societal dynamics that allowed their victimisation. Survivor testimonies are powerful; they move beyond the faceless numbers and statistics that often desensitise the public to the reality of trafficking. These voices bring immediacy and humanity to the crisis, illuminating the experiences that policy reports and official documents cannot fully capture. The testimony of a single survivor can often convey the urgency of the trafficking epidemic more effectively than pages of statistics, creating a direct emotional connection that compels society to listen and act.

Moreover, survivors, in reclaiming their narratives, hold up a mirror to Western societies, challenging them to confront the systems that perpetuate trafficking. Western societies frequently view trafficking as an external problem, relegated to impoverished nations or to underground networks that operate in the shadows. Survivor stories dismantle this illusion, revealing that trafficking occurs within Western borders, often under the guise of legitimate industries. Their voices expose the uncomfortable truth: trafficking is not solely the work of foreign criminal networks; it is also driven by domestic demand, and its victims can be found within Western borders, sometimes in plain sight.

By bringing these stories to light, survivors are not merely recounting their trauma; they are actively challenging Western societies to reassess their role in enabling this exploitation. Their testimonies force us to examine our consumption patterns, social policies, and economic practices that contribute to trafficking. They remind us that while traffickers are often the most visible perpetrators, Western societies bear collective responsibility for fuelling the demand that drives the trafficking cycle.

Here are several well-documented, public domain or freely shared survivor stories that illustrate the resilience of trafficking victims. Each narrative has been adapted from non-copyright sources and contains details shared by survivors in public records, reports, or testimonies. These accounts are selected to highlight different types of trafficking and experiences across various countries.

1. The Story of Shamere McKenzie: From Sex Trafficking Victim to Activist

Shamere McKenzie was a college student in the United States when she met a man who promised her love and a stable future. Initially unaware of his intentions, she was soon manipulated into sex trafficking, forced to endure exploitation and abuse for financial gain. After escaping her trafficker, she went on to work with various anti-trafficking organisations and openly shared her story to increase awareness about the reality of trafficking within the United States. Shamere is a key advocate for survivor-led policy reform, particularly around support services for trafficking survivors in America.

Her story reveals the psychological manipulation used by traffickers and how survivors can rebuild their lives through advocacy and support. Today, Shamere is an internationally recognised advocate, contributing to numerous panels, policy discussions, and documentaries focused on eradicating trafficking and supporting survivors.

Source: Shared publicly by Shamere McKenzie through various anti-trafficking organisations and interviews in non-copyrighted forums.

2. The Story of Somaly Mam: A Journey from Cambodian Slavery to International Activism

Born in Cambodia, Somaly Mam was sold into sex slavery as a young girl, where she endured unimaginable physical and psychological abuse. After years of exploitation, she managed to escape and later co-founded an anti-trafficking organisation to help others. Somaly has worked relentlessly to raise awareness about human trafficking, focusing on prevention, rescue, and rehabilitation for other victims within Southeast Asia.

Somaly's story, though often harrowing, emphasises the strength required to rebuild one's life and turn personal trauma into positive change. She has worked directly with hundreds of survivors and brought global attention to trafficking networks across Asia.

Source: Publicly shared by Somaly Mam in testimonies, interviews, and public talks.

3. The Story of Shandra Woworuntu: Surviving Labour Exploitation in the United States

Originally from Indonesia, Shandra Woworuntu was promised a job in the hotel industry in the United States. Upon arrival, she was instead sold into forced labour and sex trafficking. After managing to escape, she dedicated herself to helping other survivors by sharing her experiences openly, founding a non-profit focused on supporting trafficking victims. Shandra's story reflects the exploitation involved in trafficking, as well as the need for survivor-centric support systems that assist in the transition back into society.

Her experiences reveal the challenges of integration and the additional struggles faced by survivors in adapting to life post-trafficking. Shandra has since become a vocal advocate, frequently participating in legislative and community-driven efforts to combat trafficking and assist survivors.

Source: Shandra's testimony has been shared in several public forums, including survivor panels, government briefings, and open-source advocacy websites.

4. The Story of Rani Hong: From Child Trafficking Victim to U.N. Speaker

Rani Hong was trafficked from India as a child, forcibly separated from her family and sold into slavery. She endured severe abuse and isolation, eventually finding herself in forced adoption after escaping her traffickers. Today, Rani is an active voice within the United Nations, advocating for the rights of trafficking survivors and children at risk.

Her story highlights the reality of child trafficking, the long-lasting effects on victims, and the resilience required to overcome such early trauma. Through her public speeches, she aims to reshape global policies on child trafficking, offering her story as a testament to human endurance and recovery.

Source: Rani Hong's account has been widely shared in public speeches, open-source interviews, and non-copyrighted publications.

5. The Story of Tina Frundt: A Survivor and Anti-Trafficking Organisation Founder

Tina Frundt was only a teenager in the United States when she was manipulated into sex trafficking by an older man posing as a boyfriend. After surviving the ordeal, she went on to establish her anti-trafficking organisation, Courtney's House, which provides direct support to trafficking victims, focusing on children and young adults. Tina uses her experience to educate communities about trafficking prevention and has shared her story in public forums to demonstrate the importance of survivor-led support services.

Her journey from survivor to advocate highlights the importance of community awareness and direct intervention strategies. Tina's outreach and advocacy serve as an ongoing reminder of the critical role survivor voices play in both prevention and healing.

Source: Tina Frundt's story has been shared widely in open-source interviews, speeches, and public records associated with her organisation, Courtney's House.

6. The Story of Timea Nagy: Escaping Trafficking in Canada

A Hungarian national, Timea Nagy was trafficked to Canada under the false promise of legitimate employment. Once there, she was forced into sexual slavery and experienced severe abuse. After escaping, she devoted herself to advocacy work in Canada, sharing her story to raise awareness about the trafficking of migrants and the often-hidden trafficking networks within Canada.

Timea's narrative sheds light on the unique challenges faced by international trafficking victims and the need for culturally specific support in survivor recovery. She has provided testimony to influence Canadian anti-trafficking policy and has assisted in establishing various support services for survivors.

Source: Timea Nagy's testimony has been shared in non-copyrighted platforms, open testimonies, and public advocacy events in Canada.

Integrating Survivor Stories as a Call to Action

Each of these stories, shared voluntarily and publicly by the survivors themselves, illustrates the immense courage it takes to rebuild after enduring trafficking. They not only expose the brutal realities of trafficking but also bring a personal perspective to the issue that statistics alone cannot convey. Survivor testimonies serve as a powerful reminder of why society must move beyond passive empathy and towards active policy reform and survivor-centred approaches. By listening to survivors, understanding their experiences, and prioritising their voices in anti-trafficking strategies, society can develop more effective measures for preventing trafficking and supporting victims in their journey toward healing and empowerment.

From Awareness to Transformation

Acknowledging the suffering of survivors is only the first step. Real transformation requires that societies move beyond passive awareness and actively work to dismantle the structures that enable trafficking. This involves a multi-pronged approach: holding corrupt officials accountable, enforcing anti-trafficking laws across sectors, and reducing the demand for exploitative labour and services within Western markets. Survivor testimonies should guide this transformation, serving as both a moral compass and a roadmap for the changes needed to protect future generations from similar exploitation.

When society heeds the call of these testimonies, it is more likely to enact policies that truly address the root causes of trafficking. Legislation can be reformed to include protections for survivors, ensuring they have access to legal rights, employment, and support systems tailored to their unique needs. Educational initiatives can raise awareness about the realities of trafficking, from the corporate level down to consumers, fostering a collective responsibility to reduce the demand for trafficked labour and services. Survivor narratives can also inspire activism, motivating individuals and communities to advocate for changes in policy, consumer behaviour, and social attitudes that perpetuate trafficking.

In amplifying the voices of survivors, we not only honour their experiences but also lay the foundation for a more just and compassionate society. Their stories challenge us to reimagine our role in the world not as passive bystanders but as active participants in dismantling trafficking. By prioritising survivor voices in anti-trafficking initiatives, we can shift from mere empathy to meaningful action, creating a world where resilience is celebrated not because of the horrors endured but because we have collectively worked to prevent future suffering.

Reimagining Support Systems for Survivors

What becomes evident through these testimonies is the urgent need for specialised support systems within Western nations, designed specifically for survivors of human trafficking. This includes culturally sensitive mental health care, trauma-informed legal assistance, and robust social services that facilitate reintegration rather than re-traumatisation. Survivors must not only be given sanctuary but also the tools to thrive, with access to education, vocational training, and stable housing as part of a comprehensive support framework.

Without a system that genuinely addresses these needs, survivors remain in a precarious state, vulnerable to further exploitation and disenfranchisement. Acknowledging this is not merely a matter of sympathy; it is a matter of justice and reparation. These individuals, who have endured unthinkable ordeals, deserve every opportunity to rebuild their lives with dignity and agency.

The Indomitable Human Spirit

The stories in this chapter reflect not only the unspeakable brutality of human trafficking but also the indomitable spirit of those who survive it. I hope that by sharing these testimonies, I can shed light on the complex, deeply personal nature of survival, healing, and resilience.

This chapter serves as a testament to the strength of survivors and a call to all who read it to engage in the fight against trafficking with renewed vigour and commitment.

These narratives do more than illustrate resilience; they underscore the imperative to transform our understanding of trafficking and galvanise Western societies to enact meaningful change. Survivors are not mere symbols of a crisis; they are agents of their recovery, and, in their courage, they hold the power to inspire systemic transformation. Through their stories, we are reminded of both the human cost of trafficking and the urgent need for compassionate, survivor-centred solutions.

Chapter 12: Towards a Solution: Policy Recommendations and Future Directions

In the final chapter, we stand at a crucial juncture, tasked with tackling one of the darkest stains on modern civilisation human trafficking. Through the preceding chapters, I have delved into the multifaceted horrors of this crisis, exploring the intricate machinery that fuels trafficking, the profiles of victims, the role of technology, and the systemic failures that allow it to flourish. Now, having examined the various components of this pervasive trade, I turn towards a path forward. How can we confront, combat, and ultimately dismantle the human trafficking trade that infiltrates Western borders and exploits the most vulnerable members of society?

Ending human trafficking demands a comprehensive, multi-layered approach that combines strengthened border policies, improved international cooperation, and relentless prosecution of traffickers. However, it is equally crucial to address the demand driving this trade, support survivors, and re-evaluate immigration policies that sometimes inadvertently foster exploitation. In this chapter, I will outline these policy recommendations, emphasising that only through a concerted, global effort can we hope to combat the deeply rooted causes of trafficking and create a safer, more just world.

Strengthening Border Controls

As discussed in Chapter 2: The Routes to Exploitation, traffickers take advantage of long-established land, sea, and air routes to move victims undetected into the West. These pathways, which have grown increasingly sophisticated over time, exploit specific vulnerabilities in national and regional immigration systems, and their success often hinges upon the leniency and porousness of Western border policies. Open-border policies particularly in the United States have been a substantial factor in enabling traffickers to operate with alarming efficiency, blending their victims among legitimate migrants and obscuring their activities within large-scale, poorly monitored movements of people.

The remedy, therefore, is not simply more personnel or taller walls; rather, it demands an entirely reimagined approach to border security one grounded in intelligence-driven tactics and cutting-edge technology designed to track, intercept, and dismantle trafficking networks before they reach Western borders. This shift would involve collecting and utilising intelligence in real-time, allowing authorities to detect traffickers based on their unique behavioural patterns, financial transactions, and known associations, rather than relying solely on basic, reactive border checks that only scratch the surface of such a complex criminal ecosystem.

A truly sophisticated framework would integrate data from multiple agencies both domestic and international using predictive analytics, biometric recognition, and artificial intelligence to identify suspicious movements and persons who may be at risk of exploitation. For example, predictive algorithms could analyse patterns of travel, visa applications, and even encrypted communications to flag individuals associated with known trafficking networks. Given the flexibility and adaptability of traffickers, such a framework must be agile, able to respond to traffickers' tactics as they evolve, and specifically aimed at intercepting traffickers along high-traffic routes identified in prior chapters.

Further complicating the issue, open-border policies have often led to overwhelmed immigration agencies, which are forced to prioritise volume over detail in processing migrants. The sheer scale of arrivals at the US southern border, for instance, has made it nearly impossible to distinguish between legitimate asylum seekers and victims of trafficking smuggled under the guise of family reunification or refugee claims. By embedding trafficking prevention within the immigration process itself, border control agents could receive specialised training and access to data sources that would enable them to identify potential victims before they are irretrievably lost in the system.

This intelligence-driven approach must also prioritise cross-border collaborations with origin and transit countries, building a seamless flow of information that tracks traffickers across multiple borders. These partnerships are essential for creating an early-warning system one that utilises intelligence gathered from source countries to preempt traffickers long before they reach Western borders. Effective intelligence sharing would make it more challenging for traffickers to mask their movements and facilitate a global front against the trafficking trade, aligning Western nations with one another and with source nations to block traffickers' routes at every possible turn.

The crux of this effort lies in recognising that traffickers will continue to capitalise on any vulnerabilities, particularly those created by Western open-border policies until these systems are reinforced with proactive, intelligence-based solutions. The continued existence of open borders without such intelligence-driven safeguards effectively hands traffickers a roadmap, inviting them to exploit migration channels that were never intended to protect against such organised, exploitative crime. As such, a true solution to human trafficking into the West must go beyond physical barriers; it requires a complete overhaul of how borders operate, ensuring that Western countries are no longer complicit, even unwittingly, in enabling these networks.

1. **Advanced Screening and Intelligence Sharing**
   To effectively prevent trafficking at the border, Western countries must invest in technology and intelligence-sharing networks that allow for real-time data exchange among

border enforcement agencies. Collaborating with transit countries, where traffickers frequently operate, would help track and anticipate trafficking routes. For instance, partnerships with Latin American and North African nations could lead to more efficient targeting of trafficking operations before they reach Western borders.

2. **Targeted Training for Border Officials**

   Border officials need targeted training to identify potential victims of trafficking. As illustrated in *Chapter 5: The Role of Corruption*, traffickers often exploit both vulnerable migrants and the officials they encounter along transit routes. Training officials to recognise signs of coercion, falsified documents, and vulnerable travellers while adhering to anti-corruption protocols could make a substantial difference in identifying traffickers and assisting victims before they disappear into underground networks.

3. **Refined Immigration Policies**

   Immigration reform must balance the need for security with the protection of vulnerable populations. In *Chapter 8: Human Trafficking and Immigration: The Blurred Lines*, I explored how rigid immigration policies can inadvertently funnel migrants into traffickers' hands. Reform should provide legitimate pathways for migrants, reduce exploitation, and dissuade vulnerable populations from seeking perilous routes.

Improving International Cooperation

As highlighted throughout this book, human trafficking is a global problem that transcends borders. This pervasive issue cannot be effectively tackled through isolated responses from individual nations or regions. International cooperation is not merely desirable; it is essential. The transnational nature of trafficking networks means that the fight against human trafficking must involve a concerted effort from multiple stakeholders, including governments, law enforcement agencies, and civil society organisations across various countries. Each country plays a role in either facilitating or combating trafficking and thus collective action is critical to disrupting these criminal enterprises.

However, the current landscape of international cooperation is complicated by bureaucratic hurdles, particularly within the European Union (EU). The EU's open-border policies, which are mandated in all member states, create an environment that traffickers can exploit with relative ease. While the intention behind these policies may be to promote freedom of movement and economic integration, they inadvertently facilitate the movement of traffickers and their victims across member states. This situation is exacerbated by the EU's complex bureaucratic structure, which can hinder rapid responses to trafficking incidents and slow down the implementation of cohesive anti-trafficking strategies.

For instance, the processes required for coordinating law enforcement efforts across different EU nations often involve navigating a labyrinth of regulations and agreements that can delay necessary action. In many cases, national priorities differ, leading to fragmented approaches that fail to address the urgency of the trafficking crisis. This bureaucratic inertia can prevent swift and effective interventions that are essential for combatting the networks profiting from exploitation.

In contrast, the United States has witnessed a similar trend with its left-leaning open-border policies, which have been justified on various grounds, including economic benefits and humanitarian considerations. These policies, while aimed at providing pathways for vulnerable populations, have been perceived as mechanisms for garnering votes and attracting low-paid workers, which in turn raises significant concerns. By prioritising these agendas, the government has inadvertently created an environment that traffickers can exploit, leading to an increase in the number of vulnerable individuals entering the country without adequate protection. The interplay between these open-border policies and the demand for cheap labour can serve to perpetuate human trafficking, as traffickers often exploit the gaps in regulations to lure and manipulate individuals seeking better opportunities.

The intertwining of immigration policy and human trafficking highlights the necessity for a comprehensive, cooperative international framework that not only focuses on enforcement but also addresses the root causes of exploitation. Countries must work collaboratively to reform their immigration policies, ensuring they protect vulnerable migrants rather than unwittingly placing them at greater risk. This includes enhancing border security through intelligence-driven approaches while simultaneously providing pathways for legal migration that prioritise the safety and welfare of individuals.

Additionally, it is crucial for international bodies such as the EU to streamline their bureaucratic processes, enabling more effective cross-border cooperation in tackling trafficking. A unified response among EU member states would enhance the ability to share intelligence, coordinate law enforcement actions, and develop comprehensive strategies to combat trafficking at the regional level.

Ultimately, addressing human trafficking requires an understanding that no single nation can combat this issue alone. Both the EU's bureaucratic complexities and the U.S.'s open-border policies must evolve to facilitate international cooperation that effectively targets the root causes of trafficking. By fostering collaborative efforts that transcend borders, we can begin to dismantle the networks that thrive on exploitation and pave the way for a safer, more equitable future for vulnerable populations worldwide.

1. **Strengthening International Treaties and Conventions**
   While the Palermo Protocol and other treaties lay foundational guidelines for anti-trafficking, stronger, binding commitments are needed. Countries should not only sign but actively enforce anti-trafficking conventions with accountability measures in place. In *Chapter 10: The Legal Framework: International and Domestic Responses*, I critiqued the lacklustre enforcement of existing legal frameworks. An enhanced international protocol that mandates coordinated cross-border anti-trafficking initiatives would offer a formidable response to traffickers who exploit legal gaps.

2. **Creating a Centralised Anti-Trafficking Database**
   Traffickers rely on moving victims across jurisdictions, knowing that disparate data systems hinder cohesive response. By establishing a centralised database accessible to all nations, traffickers could be tracked across borders with ease, as could information about routes, trafficker profiles, and victim recovery pathways. This would streamline the process of bringing traffickers to justice, ensure that victims receive adequate support, and provide law enforcement with a more powerful tool to pre-empt trafficking operations.

3. **Deploying Task Forces in High-Risk Regions**
   Deploying international task forces in known trafficking hotspots, particularly in collaboration with countries where trafficking networks originate, could have a significant impact. For instance, task forces focused on Africa, Eastern Europe, and Southeast Asia could disrupt trafficking at its source before it reaches Western shores, leveraging local intelligence to intercept operations.

Cracking Down on Traffickers

Criminal networks lie at the heart of the trafficking industry, as illustrated in Chapter 4: The Machinery of Trafficking: Organised Crime Networks. These organisations operate with a level of sophistication and coordination that rivals legitimate businesses, utilising a myriad of resources and tactics to maintain their operations while evading law enforcement. The sheer scale and complexity of these networks present a formidable challenge to authorities seeking to dismantle them.

Understanding the structure and operations of these criminal networks is essential to developing effective strategies for intervention. At the core of many trafficking operations are hierarchical organisations, often led by individuals or small groups who orchestrate the trafficking process. These leaders typically have extensive criminal backgrounds and a keen understanding of law enforcement tactics, allowing them to stay several steps ahead of authorities. Beneath them lies a network of operatives, including recruiters, transporters, and enforcers, each playing a distinct role in the trafficking process. This layered structure makes it difficult to target these networks effectively; disrupting one segment may lead to the emergence of alternative routes and methods employed by traffickers, who are quick to adapt to any crackdowns.

In addition to their organisational complexity, these networks often transcend national borders, complicating the efforts to combat trafficking on a global scale. Traffickers frequently exploit weak governance in source and transit countries, where law enforcement may be under-resourced or corrupt, to establish safe havens for their operations. As a result, dismantling these networks requires not only national but also international cooperation. Countries must share intelligence, coordinate law enforcement actions, and harmonise legal frameworks to effectively tackle transnational trafficking networks. For instance, the establishment of joint task forces involving police and immigration officials from different countries can facilitate the pooling of resources and expertise needed to combat these complex criminal enterprises.

Furthermore, the financial aspect of trafficking cannot be overlooked. Organised crime networks generate substantial profits from their operations, often funnelling these funds into legitimate businesses or using them to bribe officials, thereby creating a cycle of corruption that sustains their activities. To disrupt these financial flows, authorities must implement stringent anti-money laundering measures and enhance their capabilities for tracking and seizing the assets of traffickers. By cutting off the financial lifeblood of these criminal networks, governments can significantly hinder their ability to recruit and exploit victims.

However, it is crucial to recognise that simply dismantling the networks is not sufficient. Authorities must also focus on addressing the underlying demand for trafficking. The very existence of these criminal organisations is sustained by a continuous influx of individuals willing to exploit vulnerable populations for profit. As discussed in Chapter 7: The Western Demand: Sex, Labour, and Exploitation, industries such as sex work, agriculture, and construction play significant roles in perpetuating trafficking. A comprehensive approach to dismantling these networks must therefore include efforts to reduce demand through public awareness campaigns, legislative changes, and support for ethical business practices.

Dismantling these networks is a formidable yet vital task. It necessitates a coordinated, multi-faceted strategy that combines law enforcement efforts with social initiatives aimed at preventing trafficking in the first place. This includes the establishment of robust victim support systems, education and awareness programmes, and community engagement initiatives that empower at-risk populations to resist exploitation. Only by taking a holistic approach can we begin to dismantle the intricate web of organised crime that sustains the trafficking industry and foster an environment where vulnerable individuals are protected from exploitation.

1. **Harsh Sentencing and Asset Seizure**
   Prosecutions alone are not enough; to deter traffickers, harsh sentencing and asset seizure laws should be standard practice. Trafficking is lucrative, and many traffickers are undeterred by the risk of prison alone. Confiscating assets would deliver a financial blow to traffickers while redistributing these funds to support victim recovery programs and anti-trafficking initiatives.

2. **Enhanced Surveillance and Investigative Powers**
   Technology has enabled traffickers to remain anonymous and evade law enforcement, as discussed in *Chapter 6: The Digital Age: How Technology Fuels Human Trafficking*. Law enforcement agencies must therefore be granted tools to monitor and infiltrate online trafficking networks. This includes permitting judicially sanctioned monitoring of suspect communications, cryptocurrency transactions, and encrypted online forums where traffickers operate.

Addressing the Demand Side

One of the most neglected yet crucial aspects of combating trafficking lies in addressing the demand. In *Chapter 7: The Western Demand: Sex, Labour, and Exploitation*, I highlighted how various industries rely on trafficked individuals to meet Western demand for cheap labour, services, and commercial sex.

1. **Consumer Awareness Campaigns**
   Consumer education is paramount. Western consumers are often unaware of how their purchases, from clothing to

agricultural goods, may be tainted by exploitation. Government and industry-sponsored awareness campaigns could encourage more ethical purchasing decisions, with labelling systems for products free of exploited labour.

2. **Regulation and Accountability of High-Risk Industries**
   Stricter regulations and audits should target industries where trafficking is prevalent. For example, mandatory audits for agricultural, construction, and domestic service sectors would ensure compliance with fair labour practices. Companies found complicit in trafficking should face severe penalties, including public sanctions and financial fines. Supply chains must be monitored rigorously, and governments should demand transparency from corporations operating in high-risk sectors.

3. **Decriminalisation of Victims in the Sex Trade**
   In the realm of the sex trade, a nuanced approach is required. Decriminalising victims while prosecuting exploiters would allow trafficking victims to seek help without fear of legal repercussions. This approach, adopted in some European nations, has shown promise by allowing law enforcement to focus on traffickers rather than prosecuting victims.

Support for Survivors

To truly support trafficking survivors, we must invest in comprehensive recovery services, which were explored through the narratives in *Chapter 11: Survivor Stories*. Survivor support is not merely a humanitarian duty; it is essential to break the cycle of exploitation.

1. **Trauma-Informed Care Programs**
   Survivors require trauma-informed care to heal from the physical and psychological scars inflicted upon them, as discussed in *Chapter 9: The Psychological and Physical Toll.*

Support programs must include counselling, medical treatment, legal assistance, and reintegration services to help survivors regain control over their lives.

2. **Educational and Employment Opportunities**
Empowering survivors with education and skills training is crucial for their long-term recovery. Without economic independence, survivors are at risk of being re-trafficked or exploited. Governments should therefore partner with NGOs to provide survivors with educational grants, job training, and employment assistance.

3. **Safe Housing and Legal Protection**
Providing survivors with secure housing and legal protections is critical. Safe housing offers a sanctuary from the traumas they have endured, while legal protections, such as temporary or permanent residency for migrant survivors, offer a sense of stability that is necessary for healing.

A Collective Call to Action

Human trafficking is a deeply entrenched and complex issue, requiring a response that is as multifaceted as the problem itself. By enhancing border security, improving international cooperation, enforcing harsher penalties on traffickers, addressing demand, and providing comprehensive support for survivors, we can start dismantling the global network that perpetuates exploitation. But we must also remember that tackling trafficking requires an unrelenting commitment from every sector governments, businesses, communities, and individuals.

In presenting these policy recommendations, I am fully aware that there is no simple solution. Yet, through sustained global collaboration, stringent policy enforcement, and compassion for survivors, we can forge a path towards a world that refuses to tolerate human trafficking.

The battle is arduous, but it is one we must wage, not only for the sake of victims but for the integrity of society itself. Let this chapter, and indeed this entire book, serve as a call to action an invitation to join the fight against an injustice that no corner of the world should ignore.

Epilogue: The Unseen Chains

As I conclude this exploration of human trafficking, it is impossible not to feel both the weight of this global crisis and a profound sense of responsibility. *Silent Slaves: The Dark Trade of Human Trafficking* has sought to shine a light into the darkest recesses of our modern world, revealing stories of harrowing exploitation, appalling violence, and the resilience of the human spirit. But for all that has been exposed, there remains so much yet unseen hidden not only by those who profit from this industry but also by the societal indifference that allows such horrors to persist.

Reflecting on the preceding chapters, I am struck by the tragic continuity of human trafficking. It is not a new evil but an ancient scourge reshaped for our times, evolving with technology, trade, and human greed. Today, it wears a different mask cloaked in the facelessness of global networks, digital anonymity, and the complexities of immigration systems. But beneath these modern guises, the crime remains as it has always been: a ruthless exploitation of human vulnerability for profit. This realisation compels us to act, and yet, as I have argued, there is no single solution to this crisis. The nature of human trafficking demands a multifaceted, coordinated response a coalition of nations, communities, policymakers, and individuals, all committed to dismantling this pernicious trade.

A Call for Human Rights-Based Policies

In *Towards a Solution*, I proposed a range of policy recommendations addressing both the supply and demand sides of human trafficking, with a focus on strengthening border controls, enhancing international cooperation, and reforming immigration laws. Each of these solutions addresses one piece of a much larger puzzle, and each is informed by the stories, data, and analyses presented throughout this book. But we must be mindful of the balance between enforcement and compassion. The fight against trafficking cannot be reduced to mere fortification of borders or sweeping reforms alone; it must be rooted in an unwavering commitment to human rights. This is particularly important for those who have been caught in the crossfire of anti-immigration measures and have found themselves more vulnerable to exploitation, not less.

I am convinced that any true solution must begin with a commitment to see trafficking victims not as numbers or collateral damage in the immigration debate, but as individuals whose human rights have been trampled. Law enforcement efforts must be as focused on protecting these victims as they are on prosecuting their abusers. Likewise, border security measures must be developed in consultation with experts on trafficking to ensure that vulnerable migrants are allowed to seek refuge and protection, rather than being inadvertently pushed into the hands of traffickers. It is a delicate balance, but one we must strive to maintain if we are to build a system that is both just and effective.

The Imperative of International Cooperation

Human trafficking is an inherently transnational issue. Borders are artificial barriers to those who operate in the shadows, navigating global markets with sophisticated networks that are remarkably adaptive. As we have seen, traffickers exploit these networks with ease, moving individuals across continents, often in plain sight. For this reason, I have called for improved international cooperation in combatting trafficking, underscoring the need for coordinated intelligence-sharing, joint operations, and standardised protocols across borders. But this requires a willingness among nations to look beyond their political differences and prioritise the common good.

While progress has been made in recent years, it remains insufficient. International organisations, governments, and NGOs must strengthen their partnerships to dismantle the complex webs of trafficking. Such partnerships must be founded on mutual trust, resource-sharing, and a common framework that ensures traffickers are pursued relentlessly. As a global community, we cannot afford to continue operating in silos, where fragmented efforts allow traffickers to exploit the gaps. The future of this fight against human trafficking lies in a world that sees such exploitation as a universal threat one that transcends political agendas and territorial disputes.

Addressing Demand and Consumer Responsibility

An uncomfortable truth underpins much of the trafficking industry: demand. Demand for cheap labour, demand for illicit services, demand for a workforce hidden from view. Western societies must confront this reality head-on, acknowledging that, while trafficking may feel distant, it often supplies the products, services, and conveniences enjoyed by millions daily. Addressing the demand side of this problem requires a shift not only in policies but in societal attitudes. We must examine our complicity in a system that fuels exploitation, whether through the purchasing decisions we make or the industries we tacitly support.

We must press industries to scrutinise their supply chains, to ensure that forced or trafficked labour is not the hidden engine driving their profits. Corporate accountability must be more than a public relations slogan; it must become a core tenet of business ethics. Consumer education, too, is a powerful tool in this fight. When individuals understand the human cost behind certain products or services, they are empowered to make more conscientious choices and decisions that support fair labour practices and ethical sourcing. By shifting demand away from exploitation, we can lessen the profitability of trafficking, thereby weakening one of its strongest pillars.

Survivor Support: Rebuilding Lives

In *Survivor Stories*, I explored the resilience of those who have endured the trauma of trafficking and emerged with their spirit unbroken. Yet survival is only the beginning. To truly combat trafficking, we must prioritise the long-term support of survivors, offering them the tools and resources necessary to rebuild their lives. This requires investment in mental health services, job training, housing, and legal assistance all of which are essential for reintegration into society.

Survivors face unique challenges, from stigma and psychological trauma to financial instability and legal hurdles. Governments, NGOs, and local communities must work in tandem to provide a support system that is both immediate and sustained. Too often, survivors are left to navigate the aftermath of their ordeal with little guidance, their needs overshadowed by the rush to apprehend their traffickers. But if we are to prevent re-trafficking and honour the dignity of these individuals, we must offer them the stability and support necessary to heal and thrive.

Looking Forward: A Shared Responsibility

Ending human trafficking requires us to acknowledge our shared responsibility. While traffickers are driven by profit and opportunity, it is society at large that provides the conditions in which this exploitation thrives. From policymakers and law enforcement to corporate leaders and ordinary consumers, each of us holds a piece of the solution. In truth, trafficking is not merely a problem for governments or NGOs to solve but a test of our collective humanity.

Silent Slaves is not merely a documentation of horror; it is a call to action. It challenges us to look beyond the statistics and see the human lives trapped in this dark trade. The solutions proposed in this book are just the beginning of what must be a long and dedicated journey. Ending human trafficking will demand sacrifice, collaboration, and an unyielding commitment to justice. It is an uphill battle, but it is a battle

we must face with courage, empathy, and an unwavering belief in the
sanctity of human dignity.

End

Did you love *Silent Slaves: The Dark Trade of Human Trafficking*? Then you should read *Influx*[1] by John Shenton!

[2]

This book presents a comprehensive exploration of one of the most pressing global issues today: mass migration. With migration influencing political, economic, and cultural dynamics across continents, the book delves into the root causes, impacts, and underlying forces behind the large-scale movement of people, particularly towards Western nations.This book provides a thought-provoking and nuanced discussion of mass migration, blending geopolitical analysis, economic investigation, and cultural insights to provide a well-rounded understanding of this complex global issue.

---

1. https://books2read.com/u/47BWMg

2. https://books2read.com/u/47BWMg

Also by John Shenton

Business Plan Basics
The Bahamas - More Islands and Recipes Than You Expect!
Collected Musings from Bricks and Mortar to E-commerce
The Smart City Odyssey: Unveiling the Secrets to Traveller-Centric
Software
The Dragon's Gambit: China's Bid for Global Dominance and the
Western Response
Silent Weapon
Business Basics: Money Sources
Influx
Fried Chips
Mandates, Motors, and Misinformation
Echos of Orwell
Control and Chaos
The Empire's Warning: What Rome's Fall Tells Us About the West
Today
Silent Slaves: The Dark Trade of Human Trafficking

About the Author

John Shenton was born in Birmingham, England and grew up in postwar England. He spent several years as a Radio Officer onboard a variety of vessels sailing to the Persian Gulf, the Indian Ocean and South China seas.

With degrees and a background in electronics and computers he has lived and worked within the United Kingdom, Germany, Switzerland and Canada.

While doing so, he established numerous trading relationships in Japan, Korea, the USA, China and other countries.

He has been retired for some time now living in Montréal Canada enjoying golfing, writing, sailing and many other things automotive.

About the Publisher

John Shenton published via Draft2digital

www.ingramcontent.com/pod-product-compliance
Lightning Source LLC
Chambersburg PA
CBHW071458140726
47997CB00005B/1770